浙江省普通本科高校"十四五"重点立项建设教材
高等院校经济管理类专业"互联网+"创新规划教材

STRATEGIC MANAGEMENT
Bilingual Teaching Case

战略管理
双语教学案例

主　编　吴　瑶　刘电光　张祺瑞
副主编　彭新敏　杨林波　王　健

内 容 简 介

本书是为配合战略管理课堂教学而设计编写的,主要采用中国本土企业实例,以双语的形式编排,及时反映中国情境特征以及企业战略管理实践的前沿动态。本书旨在通过理论与实践的结合教育,引导学生了解中国企业所处的新环境,感受国家经济蓬勃发展下的企业微观动态;提升学生运用企业战略管理理论与方法分析问题和解决问题的能力。本书编有14个案例,遵循战略管理过程框架的顺序,内容涉及战略管理的概论、内外部环境分析、战略制定和战略实施,覆盖了战略管理的主要知识点。

本书可以作为教师课堂教学参考书或者学生课后自学用书,也可以作为管理从业人员的阅读材料。

图书在版编目(CIP)数据

战略管理:双语教学案例 / 吴瑶,刘电光,张祺瑞主编. —北京:北京大学出版社,2024.3
高等院校经济管理类专业"互联网+"创新规划教材
ISBN 978-7-301-33733-2

Ⅰ.①战… Ⅱ.①吴… ②刘… ③张… Ⅲ.①企业战略—战略管理—双语教学—教案(教育)—高等学校 Ⅳ.①F272

中国国家版本馆CIP数据核字(2023)第025140号

书　　　名	战略管理:双语教学案例 ZHANLÜE GUANLI: SHUANGYU JIAOXUE ANLI
著作责任者	吴　瑶　刘电光　张祺瑞　主编
策划编辑	李娉婷
责任编辑	张　越　李娉婷
数字编辑	金常伟
标准书号	ISBN 978-7-301-33733-2
出版发行	北京大学出版社
地　　　址	北京市海淀区成府路205号　100871
网　　　址	http://www.pup.cn　　新浪微博:@北京大学出版社
电子邮箱	编辑部 pup6@pup.cn　　总编室 zpup@pup.cn
电　　　话	邮购部 010-62752015　　发行部 010-62750672　　编辑部 010-62750667
印刷者	河北滦县鑫华书刊印刷厂
经销者	新华书店
	787毫米×1092毫米　16开本　16.75印张　302千字 2024年3月第1版　2024年3月第1次印刷
定　　　价	56.00元

未经许可,不得以任何方式复制或抄袭本书之部分或全部内容。
版权所有,侵权必究
举报电话:010-62752024　电子邮箱:fd@pup.cn
图书如有印装质量问题,请与出版部联系,电话:010-62756370

前　言

本书是为配合战略管理课堂教学而设计编写的，主要采用中国本土企业实例，以双语的形式编排，及时反映中国情境特征以及企业战略管理实践的前沿动态。本书旨在通过理论与实践的结合教育，引导学生了解中国企业所处的新环境，感受国家经济蓬勃发展下的企业微观动态；提升学生运用企业战略管理理论与方法分析问题和解决问题的能力。

本书编有 14 个案例，遵循战略管理过程框架的顺序，内容涉及战略管理的概论、竞争环境分析、战略制定和战略实施，覆盖了战略管理的主要知识点。案例 1 以中国古代军事战略解释现代战略管理过程，案例 2 强调了对战略管理相关概念的理解，案例 3 是关于外部环境分析的案例，案例 4 通过引发公司的案例解释企业内部环境，案例 5 是关于竞争战略的内容，案例 6 主要讲述动态竞争战略，案例 7 是关于多元化战略的案例，案例 8 介绍了海信并购科龙的过程，案例 9 是关于国际化战略的案例，案例 10 主要讨论了京东的合作战略，案例 11 以万科为例介绍公司治理的过程，案例 12 通过对小米公司的组织结构演化强调战略与组织的关系，案例 13 主要介绍国企创业者的战略领导力，案例 14 讲述波司登的战略创业过程。每个案例都包括知识点、案例目的、案例正文、案例问题、分析提示与案例视频。

本书的编写与出版历时两年有余，编者都是来自宁波大学商学院的教师，具体分工如下：案例 1、案例 3、案例 4、案例 7 由吴瑶编写，案例 6 由陈云超、吴瑶编写，案例 9 由彭新敏编写，案例 10、案例 11、案例 12、案例 13 由张祺瑞编写，案例 2 和案例 14 由刘电光编写，案例 5 由王健编写，案例 8 由杨林波编写，全书由吴瑶统稿。案例视频分工如下：案例 1、案例 3、案例 4、案例 5、案例 6、案例 7、案例 8、案例 9 由吴瑶拍摄完成，案例 10、案例 11、案例 12、案例 13 由张祺瑞拍摄完成，案例 2 和案例 14 由刘电光拍摄完成。

本书是浙江省普通本科高校"十四五"首批新文科重点教材建设项目，本书的顺利出版也得益于宁波大学工商管理国际化专业建设项目的支持。在本书编写过程中，宁波大学硕士研究生乐海姣、李一鸣、丁洁、张瑜珊做了部分书稿校对和排版工作，北京大学出版社做了耐心细致的编辑工作，在此一并表示感谢。

本书可以作为教师课堂教学参考书或者学生课后自学用书，也可以作为管理从业人员的阅读材料。编写组成员均是来自战略管理教学一线的教师，成员们召开多次教材编写研讨会，对案例的选择、撰写风格的确定、问题设计等方面达成共识。虽然编写组认真编写、仔细校对，但能力所限，难免疏忽，本书可能还存在不完善的地方，恳请同行、读者批评指正。有任何意见或建议可联系：wuyao@nbu.edu.cn。

吴瑶
2023 年 12 月 21 日

【资源索引】

Preface

This is a case-based book intended to be used in the classroom teaching activities on strategic management. All cases are derived from local Chinese companies and drafted in both Chinese and English. These cases reflect the situational characteristics in China and the dynamics of these companies in strategic management. It is designed to guide the students to integrate theory with practice, understand the new context faced by Chinese companies, feel the micro dynamics of enterprises under the rapidly developing economy environment in China, in order to improve their ability to analyze and solve problems by applying the corporate strategy management theory and methods.

The book contains 14 cases arranged based on the strategic management process. It covers the main knowledge points of strategic management, including overview, internal and external context analysis, and strategy development and implementation. Case 1 (Longzhong Dialogue) is about strategy analysis, which discusses the modern strategic management process based on the military strategies in ancient China. Case 2 (Spring Airlines) focuses on the understanding of strategic management related concepts. Case 3 (Fenghua) is about external context analysis. Case 4 (Yinfa) is about internal context. Case 5 (Fenbi) is about competition strategy, Case 6 is about dynamic competition strategy. Case 7 gives an example of diversified strategy. Case 8 describes the process that Hisense acquired Kelon, Case 9 (Haitian) is about international strategy. Case 10 (JD.COM) mainly discusses the cooperation strategy. Case 11 discusses the corporate governance process by taking Vanke as an example. Case 12 focuses on the relationship between strategy and organization based on the evolution process of organizational structure of Xiaomi. Case 13 (ChemChina) mainly discusses the strategic leadership of SOEs, and Case 14 discusses the strategic entrepreneurship process of Bosideng. Each case includes Key points, Case Purpose, Case Description, Questions, Tips for answering the questions, QR code for case video.

It took more than two years to prepare and publish the book. All writers participating in the book are the teachers from the School of Business of Ningbo University. In particular, Cases 1, 3, 4, and 7 are written by Wu Yao, Case 6 by Chen Yunchao and Wu Yao, Case 9 by Peng Xinmin, Cases 10, 11, 12, and 13 by Zhang Qirui, Cases 2 and 14 by Liu Dianguang, Case 5 by Wang Jian, and Case 8 by Yang Linbo. The book was finally compiled and edited by Wu Yao. Videos of Cases 1, 3, 4, 5, 6, 7, 8 and 9 by Wu Yao, videos of Cases 10, 11, 12, 13 by Zhang Qirui, videos of Cases 2 and 14 by Liu Dianguang.

This textbook is the result of the first batch of key new liberal arts textbooks construction projects for ordinary undergraduate universities in Zhejiang Province during the 14th Five Year Plan period. For the publication of this book, the Business Administration Internationalization Program of Ningbo University provided great support and Peking University Press carried out careful and patient editing work. Besides, the post graduates of Ningbo University Le Haijiao, Li Yiming, Ding Jie, and Zhang Yushan carried out a lot of proofreading and typesetting work. I would like to express my appreciation for them.

The book may be used as a reference by teachers, students as well as management personnel. All the writers of the cases are front line teachers engaged in strategic management. We held several discussions on the case selection, writing style, and questions design. Despite of our full efforts and careful editing, inadequacy is inevitable due to limited proficiency. Any criticism and suggestions from the peers and readers are appreciated. For any comments, please contact: wuyao@nbu.edu.cn

Wu Yao

December 21, 2023.

目　　录

案例 1　《隆中对》的战略管理思想简读 1

案例 2　春秋航空：廉价航空的春秋大业 7

案例 3　风华物业：顺势而为下的战略转型 13

案例 4　站在转型升级十字路口的引发公司 19

案例 5　粉笔公考的竞争战略 27

案例 6　三家企业在甲醇钠产品上的动态竞争较量 35

案例 7　多元化：红帮裁缝的岔路口 45

案例 8　企业并购中的整合：海信与科龙 53

案例 9　海天：把产品覆盖到有海有天的地方 61

案例 10　京东的合作战略 71

案例 11　万科的公司治理之路 79

案例 12　小米公司的组织结构演化 91

案例 13　国企创业家任建新与中国化工 101

案例 14　羽绒国货波司登的战略性创业之路 109

Case 1   A Brief Analysis of Longzhong Dialogue's Strategic Management Thoughts 117

Case 2   Spring Airlines: the Great Cause of Low-cost Airlines 125

Case 3   Fenghua Property: Strategic Transformation Following the Trend 133

Case 4   Yinfa: A Company in A Dilemma of Transformation and Upgrading 139

Case 5   Competitive Strategy of Fenbi (A Platform for Civil Servant Examination Training) 149

Case 6   Dynamic Competition Among Three Companies on Sodium Methoxide 159

Case 7   Hong Bang Tailors at a Crossroads of Diversification 175

Case 8   The Integration of Enterprises in M&A: HISENSE's Acquisition of KELON 185

Case 9   Haitian: Sell Products to Places Throughout the World 193

Case 10   The Cooperative Strategies of JD.com 205

Case 11   Corporate Governance Evolution of Vanke 215

Case 12   The Organization-Structural Evolution of Xiaomi 231

Case 13   Ren Jianxin, the Founder of ChemChina 243

Case 14   Strategic Entrepreneurship of Bosideng—A Domestic Brand in Down Garment Industry 253

案例 1

《隆中对》的战略管理思想简读

知识点：

战略管理过程、环境与战略的适配性

案例目的：

本案例通过对《隆中对》中蕴含的战略管理思想进行分析，引导学生理解战略管理过程，思考环境与战略的适配性。

案例正文：

自董卓已来，豪杰并起，跨州连郡者不可胜数。曹操比于袁绍，则名微而众寡，然操遂能克绍，以弱为强者，非惟天时，抑亦人谋也。今操已拥百万之众，挟天子而令诸侯，此诚不可与争锋。孙权据有江东，已历三世，国险而民附，贤能为之用，此可以为援而不可图也。荆州北据汉、沔，利尽南海，东连吴会，西通巴、蜀，此用武之国，而其主不能守，此殆天所以资将军，将军岂有意乎？益州险塞，沃野千里，天府之土，高祖因之以成帝业。刘璋暗弱，张鲁在北，民殷国富而不知存恤，智能之士思得明君。将军既帝室之胄，信义著于四海，总揽英雄，思贤如渴，若跨有荆、益，保其岩阻，西和诸戎，南抚夷越，外结好孙权，内修政理；天下有变，则命一上将将荆州之军以向宛、洛，将军身率益州之众出于秦川，百姓孰敢不箪食壶浆以迎将军者乎？诚如是，则霸业可成，汉室可兴矣。

——摘自陈寿《三国志·蜀书·诸葛亮传》

1800多年前，刘备三顾茅庐去请诸葛亮出山，第三次诸葛亮答应刘备出山，并向刘备提出了被后人称为《隆中对》的战略规划。

首先，诸葛亮向刘备分析了当时的市场竞争环境：各大企业都想占领市场份额，竞争异常激烈。

其次，诸葛亮分析了竞争对手曹操的情况。曹操是宦官养子，虽家境富贵，但名声不大。相比于袁绍来说，曹操实力很弱、资源很差、队伍也不强。但是他能从一个弱者成长为一个强者，并不单纯是因为他抓住了机遇，而是他有战略、谋略。曹操的实力非常强大，在市场竞争中属于强势龙头企业。因此，诸葛亮建议刘备不要与他正面冲突。

然后，诸葛亮分析了竞争对手孙权的情况。孙权长期占据江东市场，市场基础好、顾客忠诚度高、兵精粮多，而且江东市场地势险要，有长江为天然屏障。虽然孙权也是竞争对手，但是刘备可以先和孙权结盟，合力抗曹。

在分析了市场竞争环境后，诸葛亮给出了两个突破口——荆州和益州。荆州地理位置优越，四通八达。而目前占据这个市场的刘表实力比较弱，且顾客忠诚度不高。诸葛亮在为刘备分析战略局势的时候，指出外部环境中的威胁，即竞争对手很强大，外部的竞争很激烈，但是外部环境中也存在突破口，这个突破口就是还没有被别人牢牢掌控的荆州。他接着指出另外一个突破口——益州。益州沃野千里，是很大的市场，曾经有企业占领于此，成就过一番大事业。但现在占据益州的是刘璋。刘璋拥有很好的人才，却没有给他们提供相应的发展平台，导致很多人才想要跳槽，希望能到优秀的企业中施展抱负。

在分析完外部环境后，诸葛亮转向分析内部环境。刘备具有以下资源和能力："帝室之胄"，说明企业有一个老字号品牌；"信义著于四海"，说明刘备带领的团队是有很好的声誉的，企业美誉度高；"总揽英雄，思贤如渴"，说明刘备的军队具有好的人力资源。

在分析了外部环境和内部环境之后，诸葛亮给刘备指了一条战略路径：做好内部管理，到外面去与孙权结盟；通过跟周边的一些部队搞好关系，占领荆州和益州；夺取荆州和益州之后，荆州、益州互为照应，对曹操形成钳制，从而实现一统天下之局面。"诚如是，则霸业可成，汉室可兴矣"这正是刘备的愿景和使命。

《隆中对》是一个非常经典的战略规划报告。在《隆中对》中，诸葛亮指出了企业的愿景、使命和战略目标——"成霸业，兴汉室"，围绕这个目标，先进行外部环境、市场环境和竞争环境分析；再进行关于资源和能力的内部环境分析，找出机会、威胁、优势、劣势；最后制定战略：夺取荆州和益州，并以此为根据地，结盟孙权合力对抗曹操，以实现战略目标。

也正是在《隆中对》的指引下，让当时内忧外患的刘备，通过一系列战役，成就了一番伟业。然而，再完美的战略规划也要因时而变。孙权和刘备的结盟瓦解、兵力过于分散等因素使刘备只实现了《隆中对》一半的战略目标。

案例问题：

1.《隆中对》中的战略管理过程包含哪些内容？

2.诸葛亮在向刘备提出结盟孙权、夺取荆州和益州的战略路径是出于什么考虑？

3."成霸业，兴汉室"的战略目标并没有完全实现，你认为原因是什么？

4.你认可诸葛亮在《隆中对》中所提出的战略思路吗？如何评价？

分析提示：

1.战略管理过程包括愿景、使命、战略目标、内部和外部环境分析、战略制定、战略实施与调整，是一个闭环的过程。

2.战略路径是在环境分析和战略制定的基础上提出来的。环境分析包括外部环境分析和内部环境分析。企业需要识别出外部环境中的机会和威胁，结合内部环境中的优势和劣势，找到战略制定的方向，在战略突破口中确定战略路径。

3.学生可以结合当时刘备所处的内、外部环境进行分析，并考虑环境的动态性。当环境发生改变时，战略也需要进行相应的调整。战略目标的达成与否和企业所处的环境及环境的变化密不可分。

4.战略管理者需要在变化的环境中，预测、适应甚至是创造变化，并在变化中取得企业竞争的胜利。战略管理者的战略决策与当时所处的情境有关，也与战略管理者对于环境的把握和判断有关。学生可以结合当时的情境，形成自己对战略问题的判断。

案例 2

春秋航空：廉价航空的春秋大业

知识点：

行业环境、竞争优势、战略、战略实施、战略领导者、使命、愿景、组织文化、战略管理过程

案例目的：

本案例通过对春秋航空所处环境及其战略的分析，引导学生理解使命、愿景和战略实施，思考战略领导者发挥的重要作用。

案例正文：

2020年暴发的新冠肺炎疫情使全球航空业深陷旋涡，随之而来的出行需求疲软、运力不足、现金流短缺等持续性影响，令航空业被迫面临新一轮洗牌。然而，2021年廉价航空则率先恢复到疫情之前的水平，并取得新的成长。其中，春秋航空作为中国廉价航空先行者，其出色表现令人刮目相看。

在人们的传统观念中，航空出行是一项奢侈的选择，甚至是专属于商务人士等高端消费群体的"特权"。而从市场来看，中国航空业一直以来也只有南方航空、东方航空、中国国际航空等几家大型国有航空公司，其所提供的基本都是高价位的全服务航空。

2006年，为了打破上述局面，春秋航空相继推出"1元""99元""199元""299元"等超低票价。2013年，中国民航局与国际民航组织召开了中国低成本航空的发展和未来峰会，标志着飞机从"非富即贵"的享受工具向"人人可用"的运载工具转变，航空出行不再是身份显赫、豪华奢侈的象征。

廉价航空，又称低成本航空，是指一些航空公司在满足飞行安全标准的前提下，通过将一些传统航空包含于票价中的服务进行剥离，有偿提供除了航空位移的服务，从而降低公司运营成本、降低常规票价、吸引更多旅客，达到持续经营的目的。廉

价航空以低票价为基础，坚持薄利多销，从根本上改变了传统航空的市场结构。如今，廉价航空已经席卷全球主要航空市场，成为航空业中发展最快的领域之一。

20世纪70—80年代，70%～80%的欧洲中短航程业务属于廉价航空。近年来，廉价航空的发展迅速。一方面，欧洲老牌航空公司，如欧洲三大航（英航、汉莎、法航）都剥离了廉价航空事业部，独立开展欧洲中短航程业务。另一方面，全世界廉价航空蓬勃发展，涌现出一批杰出的廉价航空企业，如美国西南航空、巴西戈尔航空、中国春秋航空等。

从世界范围比较来看，中国的廉价航空市场虽然起步晚、现有市场份额尚小，但是潜在需求极其庞大，正在迎来爆发性增长。中国的廉价航空公司主要包括春秋航空、九元航空、成都航空、西部航空、幸福航空、乌鲁木齐航空和祥鹏航空等。

春秋航空从2005年7月正式投入商业运营以来，坚持低成本战略，奉行"让人人都能飞"的理念，至今保持盈利。截至2023年9月，春秋航空已拥有122架空客A320系列飞机，平均机龄7.0年，航点覆盖了中国、东南亚、东北亚的主要商务和旅游城市，经营航线210余条，年运输旅客2000万人次。春秋航空之所以能取得骄人的业绩，是因为清晰的竞争战略。在国内大部分航空公司缺乏明确的市场定位、仍然笼统地将旅客"一把抓"的时候，春秋航空就已经着眼于廉价航空市场，服务于大众了。

为了有效贯彻低成本战略，春秋航空坚持采用"两单""两高""两低"的经营策略，通过占据国内支线市场、运用自主营销渠道、对旅客提供差异化服务，进而实现扩张和盈利。"两单"是指单一机型和单一舱位。春秋航空的机型为空客A320，通过改装，取消了头等舱、商务舱，只提供经济舱。相比于两舱制，单一机型、单一舱位的机队规模和客舱布局降低了人员培训、航材储备、维修等成本。"两高"是指高客座率和高飞机利用率。春秋航空的飞机通过改装，座位数量增加到186个，比国内一般客机多26个座位。这使平摊到每位旅客的成本就减少了14%～15%。为了实现高飞机利用率，春秋航空采用"点对点"的航线结构，高密度地编排航班。例如，厦门、沈阳、哈尔滨、青岛、广州、海口、三亚等航线每天开通2～4个航班。"两低"则是指低营销费用和低管理费用,包括:简化地面和客舱服务;减轻免费行李重量;依靠春秋国旅的网点、采用电话呼叫中心、网上直销等方式订票,尽可能地减少人力成本和运营费用。

春秋航空董事长王正华有一句口头禅:"钱一半是赚的,一半是省的。"在春秋航空的成本节约方面,王正华"节俭经营"的模式已成为行业标杆。在这样的管理模式下,春秋航空的主营业务成本比行业平均水平低62%,管理成本比行业平均水平低50%,财务成本比行业平均水平低60%,营销成本比行业平均水平低78%。对于春秋航空的企业战略,王正华认为,第一是要了解自己的优势,找准定位;第二是要持之以恒。

王正华曾经率队到英国、美国等国家的廉价航空公司实地考察,全面借鉴国外廉价航空公司的经验,充分挖掘与核心客运业务相关的辅助业务潜力。春秋航空辅助业务主要包括机供品销售、逾重行李收费、快速登机和保险佣金等。2022年,春秋航空实现辅助业务收入4.9亿元。

结合中国航空业的情况,春秋航空探索出了新的经验。春秋航空投入近2000万元研发自己的售票系统,鼓励旅客到公司官网上购票。公司官网会经常举办机票的促销活动。为方便旅客购票,春秋航空还与支付宝、微信支付及各大银行开展合作。另外,春秋航空还开发出离港系统。离港系统由旅客值机系统和航班控制系统组成,通过该系统,航空公司可以完成旅客的选座、登记等工作。旅客也可以在家中自助购票、选座,不用办理行李托运手续。春秋航空还推出了"99系列"特价机票以吸引目标客户群,提高客户的忠诚度和满意度。2013年,当国内大多数中小航空公司仍然依赖传统的票务代销渠道时,春秋航空凭借独立电子系统节省了超过2.8亿元的费用。春秋航空销售系统的应用最大限度地减少了机票销售过程中的代理费用和其他相关费用,增强了销售的独立性与销售渠道的掌控力,维持着较高的机票直销比例。与此同时,春秋航空通过利用第三方服务商在各地机场的资源与服务,尽可能地降低日常管理费用。例如,春秋航空只有5个管理层级,最大限度地简化了人员关系。在节约大量人力成本的同时,提高了企业的凝聚力。同时,通过严格的预算管理、科学的绩效考核，以及人机比的合理控制，春秋航空还有效降低了管理人员的人力成本和日常费用。

【案例2】

案例问题：

1. 在航空业中，环境对于航空公司绩效的影响体现在哪些方面？根据产业组织（I/O）模型，分析春秋航空如何获取超额利润，并分享你的理解。

2. 创始人王正华对春秋航空的战略有哪些重要影响？在航空业中，战略领导者如何才能取得成功？

分析提示：

1. 超额利润的 I/O 模型可以解释外部环境对公司战略行动的决定性影响。I/O 模型强调，与管理者做出的组织内部的决定相比，公司选择进入的细分行业对业绩产生的影响更大。在本案例中，面对国内航空出行的庞大需求，春秋航空选择了廉价航空战略并获得超额利润。学生可以在考察外部环境、行业结构特点、自身资源优势的基础上，对春秋航空的公司战略及其所获得的超额利润展开分析。

2. 战略领导者是指那些来自公司不同部门和不同层级的，用战略管理过程来选择战略行动，并帮助公司实现愿景、履行使命的人。战略领导者对公司的影响是全方位的，他不仅主导着公司战略的大方向，而且其个人的决策和行动也会影响组织文化的塑造。在本案例中，春秋航空创始人王正华是一位战略领导者。学生可以围绕王正华的言行，对其把握外部环境、决策公司战略、塑造企业文化等行为展开分析。

案例来源：

1. 孙睿，等. 匠心神兵——春秋航空的峥嵘与未来. 中国管理案例共享中心案例.

2. 春秋航空上市公司年报（2013—2022 年）.

案例 3

风华物业:顺势而为下的战略转型

知识点：

宏观环境、产业环境、竞争环境

案例目的：

本案例通过介绍风华物业董事长给股东的一封信，引导学生分析外部环境中的宏观环境、产业环境和竞争环境，思考环境与战略的适配问题。

案例正文：

风华物业有限公司董事长致股东的一封信

在公司成立 30 周年之际，风华物业有限公司（以下简称风华物业）董事长给股东写了一封信，信的内容如下。

我们公司作为本地第一家物业管理企业，自 1991 年 5 月成立以来，经过 30 年的发展，物业管理面积近 1 亿平方米，拥有员工 18000 多人，进入全国物业百强榜。发展中，我们形成了具有较高知名度的区域品牌，团队在共同经历艰苦奋斗中更加团结，忠诚度更高。目前，公司实施的全国化战略使我们的市场版图从本地走向了全国。业务类型包括办公楼、政府机关、高层住宅、高档别墅、商业广场、城市综合体、工业区、景区等多元化的物业类型，发展的速度与规模已经非昔日所能比。

公司之所以能取得今天的成绩，主要是因为对外部环境始终保持高度的敏感性和灵活性，敢于变革、适时转型。公司在创立之初主要面向传统的住宅物业，转型后定位中高端住宅物业，当时适逢房地产市场发展处于上升期，公司承接了一些本地的住宅项目，在市场上逐渐站稳脚跟。后来，随着本地房地产形势的不断攀升，外来地产商大量涌入，本地企业难以招架，这些外来企业自带的物业项目迅速挤占了住宅物业的市场空间。当政府提出"楼宇经济"时，公司就顺势而为，开拓写字楼业务，开始了从"住宅业务"向"商务楼宇"的第一次转型。当时，写字楼业务也是公司的招牌业务，给公司带来了可观的收益。但是后来由于新竞争者的涌入，加上写字楼供应过剩、物业费回收困难等，迫使公司不得不又一次转型。在政府提出"服务外包"的契机下，公司及时把握住机遇，承接了大量政府服务项目，开始了从"商务楼宇"向"城市服务"的第二次转型。目前，风华物业住宅业务收入只占总业务收入的10%，以政府楼宇、公众物业为主的城市服务业务逐年上升，成为公司主要业务收入的来源。

在此基础上，公司提出了"城市服务商"的定位。这次转型公司面临更多的机遇和更大的挑战。从机遇上来看，一方面，政府的服务外包业务范围还将逐步扩大，对业务的经营和盈利点还有很大的想象空间；另一方面，我国城市服务竞争尚不激烈，还是一片可以去争夺的蓝海。从挑战上来看，一方面，在房地产已经由增量市场进入存量市场的背景下，大量的物业企业纷纷将竞争的触角转向公共服务或者城市服务领域，依靠资本和科技的力量开始从传统物业服务向现代物业服务转型，不断发掘物业增值服务的价值。这些地产大鳄下属的物业企业承受风险能力和开拓能力极强，对新出现的市场虎视眈眈。例如，碧桂园服务已与遵义、衡水、西昌等多个城市达成战略合作，并持续推进项目落地。另一方面，一些依托互联网、高科技的专业化公司，定位清晰、市场明确，在专业化服务、增值业务拓展、项目经营等方面具有很强的优势。

目前公司的业务增速快，是因为选对了市场转型的方向——做城市服务商，但这个市场的红利我们还能享用多久？高速的扩张掩盖了很多发展中的问题。公司的收入虽然逐年增长，但利润率却没有明显提升。这些挑战是公司在进入城市服务商领域必须要思考和面对的问题。

相较于传统的物业领域，城市服务包括了更多业态，它不仅包括对传统的小区、办公楼的服务，还包括对学校、医院、景区、高速公路等跟城市运营有关的服务。也就是说，一个城市运营所需要的一切服务都是公司的业态。业务范围大大拓展了，竞争格局也发生了巨大的变化。但是到底什么是城市服务商？这仍然是值得大家共同思考的问题。

案例问题：

1. 风华物业在 30 多年的发展历程中经历了哪些战略转型？

2. 风华物业在向城市服务商转型的过程中面临哪些外部环境中的机会和威胁？

3. 结合案例说明为什么企业研究和了解外部环境是非常重要的。

分析提示：

1. 风华物业的每一次战略转型都伴随着外部环境的改变。结合案例资料，学生可以梳理出外部环境的几次变化，以及与之对应的企业战略转型，思考战略与环境的关系。风华物业的战略转型可以从业务内容和范围的转型升级考虑。

2. 风华物业在向城市服务商的转型的过程中也遇到了一些机会和挑战，可以从外部环境中的宏观环境、产业环境和竞争环境等方面展开分析。城市服务商是指物业企业承接政府委托项目，以服务城市管理、运营为目的开展物业服务活动。学生需要思考一些物业企业逐步加大城市服务业务的开拓，背后受到哪些外部环境因素的影响。

3. 回顾案例分析过程以及在外部环境分析中关于所用到的波特五力分析模型、动态竞争模型等工具和方法，进一步理解环境的动态性，以及战略与环境的适配性。

案例来源：

本案例是编者根据企业实地调研及网上公开数据整理改编而得。

案例 4

站在转型升级十字路口的引发公司

知识点：

内部环境分析、核心能力、核心资源、价值－稀缺－难以模仿－组织（VRIO）模型

案例目的：

案例研究对象是处于战略抉择困惑中的宁波引发绿色食品有限公司，通过对企业发展历程的描述，引导学生思考企业所具备的内部资源与能力，识别企业存在的优势和劣势，了解内部环境与企业战略的适配性。

案例正文：

1. 引言

2018年12月11日，宁波引发绿色食品有限公司（以下简称引发公司）创始人王勇（化名）的女儿王艳（化名）和女婿赵锦（化名）在宁波股权交易中心（以下简称甬股交）共同敲锣，标志公司正式挂牌甬股交，融资能力将进一步增强，综合经营水平、市场影响力和美誉度也将进一步提升。对于大部分宁波本地企业而言，甬股交在中介机构介入程度、信息披露要求等方面更加接地气，通过在甬股交的培育孵化，为将来走向新三板和首次公开发行（IPO）打下坚实的基础。

王勇11岁就辍学跟着父母种雪菜、腌雪菜、卖咸齑。这些技能让他成为"咸齑"的省级非物质文化遗产传承人，并帮助他将引发公司发展为宁波农业龙头企业。然而不算太高的产值和较低的行业门槛始终制约着引发公司的发展壮大。从国外留学归来的女儿和女婿给引发公司的发展带来了一些新的思路，他们响应国家乡村振兴的号召，创办了艾农星创天地，希望通过农业孵化器的建设引进创新之源。

2. 企业内部资源

（1）实物资源

经过多年的技术沉淀与市场推广，引发公司已经发展成为一家集研发、种植、加工、销售为一体的综合型食品加工企业，主要有酱腌菜、调味料、淀粉制品、谷物粉类制成品和罐头。引发公司厂区占地 56 亩，厂房面积 30000 平方米，拥有 2000 亩雪里蕻种植基地，车间内拥有一系列完整的腌渍蔬菜产线。目前，引发公司在厂房、车间、设备等资源上还有空余。

（2）财务资源

引发公司的财务资源以企业初期创办者的出资及多年同类产品的销售强者地位作为底气。2018 年，引发公司农产品产值达 3000 万元，其中雪菜、梅干菜占 70%，在这一细分市场领域在全国占据领先地位。

（3）技术资源

雪菜作为引发公司的主打产品之一，其原料的种植要经历科学选种、适时种植、合理施肥、精细采收等多个步骤，需要优质的土壤和气候。在多年传承的腌制工艺的基础上，引发公司的研发人员对腌制工艺进行了不断钻研、改良和更新。如今，随着时代的变迁，人们在怀念家乡风味的同时，口味可能会发生变化。而引发公司的腌制工艺在保留原始口味的同时也在不断改良。

（4）企业文化及形象

引发公司作为非物质文化遗产项目"邱隘咸齑腌制技艺"的传承单位，有独特的企业文化。他们将"用心制作有浓郁地方特色的美食，使之经久流传"作为使命，将"品质是生存之本，敏捷行动，精简经营，重视劳动和勤勉的价值"作为经营理念。王勇发现人们对腌制品存在一定的偏见和误解，为了弘扬雪菜文化、传承咸齑腌制技艺，同时告诉人们合理制作的腌制品并没有想象中的危害，而是味道可口的健康食品，王勇用这项腌制技艺申报了非物质文化遗产，并全资建设了宁波"鄞州雪菜博物馆"作为引发公司独特的文化标识。引发公司每年接待大量合作方或游客参观，并积极举办雪菜文化节，邀请市民一起参加，也会经常与政府合作举办一些非物质文化遗产活动来宣传雪菜文化。这些活动也带动了引发公司的发展。

（5）人力资源

引发公司目前拥有职工总人数120人，其中管理人员13人、技术人员5人和车间工人102人。引发公司面临专业农业技术人员缺乏的问题，这也导致了近几年引发公司无法在技术上有进一步的革新。通过对引发公司内部员工年龄分布的调查，发现员工年龄分布较平衡，都集中在30～50岁，其中技术人员年龄集中在30～40岁，84.6%的管理人员年龄在30～40岁，55%的车间工人年龄在40～50岁，20～30岁的员工数量为零。

3. 以雪菜为核心的利基战略

引发公司以健康为导向，以绿色为标志，以传承为手段，以雪菜、梅干菜和虾片系列为主打产品。雪菜和梅干菜主要提供给餐饮行业的中央厨房如快餐店的后厨，作为烧菜时辅助的配料。因为雪菜是宁波的地方特色蔬菜，在市场的消费区域上具有局限性，所以它的消费群体大部分集中在江浙沪，在其他区域的销售量较小。整个腌制品市场也因为可替代品（如萝卜干）的出现，以及大家对腌制品健康担忧而慢慢地萎缩。因而基于利基战略，往纵深方向发展雪菜和梅干菜，引发公司推出了以这两类腌制品为底料的调味料产品——用以雪菜或梅干菜作为调料与食材一起煮。调味料产品的优势是简单方便。目前，引发公司已经开发出了五种调味料产品，分别为炒肉萝卜干、煮鱼酸菜、蒸鱼雪菜、烧肉梅干菜（桂花冰糖）和烧肉梅干菜（鲜香咸味）。

引发公司雪菜的优势在于原料的高质量和公司自身的文化优势。引发公司的腌制雪菜都是用严格按照要求种植的优质雪菜做的，市场反馈较好。除此之外，引发公司弘扬雪菜文化，建立博物馆，积累了独特的文化资源。

4. 以星创天地为载体的平台战略

星创天地是众创空间在农村基层的一种表现形式，是对星火计划的一种传承和发扬。星创天地简言之是"星火燎原、创新创业，科技顶天，服务立地"，既是农业科技创新创业服务平台，又是新型职业农民的"学校"和创新型农业企业家的"摇篮"，是农村科技创新创业服务体系的重要组成部分，是推行科技特派员创制度的重要举措。星创天地为农村创新创业提供良好环境，降低创业门槛，减少创业风险。相对于星火计划，星创天地在服务对象、服务内容、服务方式等方面有了进一步提升，从服务"传统农业和传统农民"向服务"现代农业和新型职业农民"转变；从示范推广"短、平、快"的实用技术向转移转化"高、新、特"的农业高新技术转变；从"科技研发管理"向"创新服务"转变；从"输出一人、致富一家"的加法向"一人创业、致富一方"的乘法转变；从"推进农村工业化进程"的目标向"促进农村一二三产业融合、产城产镇产村融合发展"的目标转变。星创天地作为以企业为主体、市场为导向的农村科技创新服务体系重要组成部分，为农业农村创新创业提供全方面的服务，构建"创业苗圃＋孵化器＋加速器"的创新创业孵化服务链条。除了在专业领域深耕，引发公司于2017年进入科技部公示的全国第二批星创天地建议备案名单里，开始了对农业孵化的探索。

引发公司对孵化器配置有专门的管理人员，想通过引入这一平台来寻找突破口，将闲置的厂房和场地租赁给园区内的初创企业，并为初创企业提供加工、包装设计等服务。引发公司用新的盈利方式，改变以扩大产品销售为核心的企业运营要素，增加了竞争优势。引发公司实行平台战略，优势是配套的食堂、住宿和场地的租赁费用都比较便宜，并有闲置的厂房、设备和场地。引发公司还将宁波鄞州区农民合作经济组织联合会引进来，与星创天地的技术平台、交易平台和服务平台相结合，提供了更多的技术指导。也就是说，初创企业可以通过引发公司的孵化器平台以更低的价格完成产品生产、加工和包装，并获得技术指导，以更少的成本生产更优质的产品。通过农业孵化器平台，引发公司可以吸引各方面的资源与力量，促进农业生产组织方式从粗放型向集约高效型转变，实现资源优化配置，让闲置的设备和场地也能实现价值，最终推动农业转型升级，提高了自身的竞争优势，更有利于公司的长久发展。因为引发公司所处位置偏远，所以目前招商情况不是特别理想。而且引发公司主要想引进农产品企业，但目前引进的主要是中药保健类和园艺类的企业，与预想存在差异。

引发公司是选择纵深方向发展战略围绕雪菜进行价值链延伸，还是选择平台化发展战略开拓更多的市场空间，这是一个艰难的决定。目前引发公司选择两者并行，但长此以往两者是否能兼顾？有限的资源更应投向哪个领域才能使引发公司真正转型成功？这是一个摆在引发公司战略决策层面前的重要问题。

案例问题：

1. 引发公司在面临战略选择时，其内部环境有哪些重要作用？
2. 引发公司有哪些有形资源和无形资源？
3. 引发公司的资源和能力中有哪些能帮助企业构建核心竞争力？运用VRIO模型识别引发公司内部资源和能力上存在的优势和劣势。

分析提示：

1. 这个问题是关于内部环境分析的重要性。企业要发展持续竞争优势，就必须获取、捆绑和利用各种资源。从企业内部环境分析是为了决定如何通过对现有的、有限的资源进行配置和整合，实现竞争优势的发挥和强化，为顾客创造更大的价值。

2. 理解有形资源和无形资源的概念与内涵。有形资源是指能够用价值指标或货币指标直接衡量，具有实物形态或能够看得见并明确界定其数量的资产。无形资源是指能够为组织创造收益，但不具有独立实物形态的资产。

3. 核心竞争力是指居于核心地位，能使组织超越竞争对手并获得较大利润的要素作用力。可以帮助企业获得核心竞争力的内部资源有四个标准：有价值的、稀缺的、难以模仿的、能被组织利用的。

案例来源：

本案例是编者根据企业实地调研及网上公开数据整理改编而得。

案例 5

粉笔公考的竞争战略

知识点：

波特五力分析模型、企业资源与能力分析、集中差异化战略

案例目的：

通过本案例的学习，加强学生对宏观环境分析、资源分析、核心竞争力分析，及波特五力分析模型等战略工具的理解和运用，理解竞争战略的基本形式及适用条件。

案例正文：

1. 粉笔公考的崭露头角

2013年，张小龙担任北京粉笔蓝天科技有限公司（以下简称粉笔）的CEO，粉笔开始在其平台开展公务员考试在线培训。2013—2014年，粉笔公务员考试栏目营业收入500万元，其中各课程收入在50万~60万元。

虽然课程种类多，任务繁重，但张小龙不愿降低服务质量。2014年，粉笔五人的公务员考试队伍只剩三人，这种情况迫使张小龙团队决定只开一个班。选择什么样的课程，是困扰张小龙团队的一个问题。基于用户的角度，张小龙最终选择做一个系统班。但如何给系统班定价是另一个问题。当时，线下公务员考试培训课程的价格相对昂贵。张小龙认为，要想打败公务员考试线下培训机构，就必须表现出与众不同。既然是在线教育，价格就要远低于线下培训的市场价。当时华图班的价格为2000元左右，张小龙团队把系统班的价格定为680元。定好价格后，张小龙团队担心价格超出用户预期，用户不太愿意购买；价格太低于用户预期，会让用户产生便宜没好货的消极心理。但事实上，系统班的销量非常好。

2015年，粉笔系统班的销量仍保持快速增长的趋势。这时张小龙团队里有人提

出可以增加其他课程来获取更多利润。也有网友建议粉笔增加冲刺班和问答班。因此，张小龙团队决定加一个 90 元的冲刺班。冲刺班单独销售，但它也作为礼品赠送给购买系统班的用户。2015 年上半年，粉笔冲刺班的营业收入达 100 万元，利润达到 90 万元以上。增加冲刺班后，粉笔短期内确实增加了利润，但又出现了新的问题，如系统班的销量下降、考试通过率降低等，这会影响口碑。而且冲刺班的服务流程不如系统班。考虑到这些因素，张小龙团队毅然放弃了冲刺班。

之后，张小龙团队就将精力和资源放在系统班上，并根据用户的反馈积极改进产品。2015—2016 年，粉笔公务员考试市场发展良好。很多人建议张小龙提高系统班的价格，但张小龙团队不同意，并且不断优化产品。

最初，粉笔只做在线教育，但学生们希望能够配备纸质的讲义，于是张小龙团队决定出配套讲义。他们选择了最好的纸张，甚至添加了保护用户视力的添加剂。为了增强讲义的风格，他们选择了线缝方法。此外，为了提高视觉舒适度，他们还请专业的设计工作室来设计讲义的封面和文字排版。因为这些细节导致成本的增加，所以张小龙团队决定将课程定价提高 200 元。张小龙团队担心涨价会影响销售。不过粉笔的口碑非常好，涨价对用户的积极性没有太大影响。2017 年，粉笔营业收入突破 1 亿元，固定用户 30 万人，在公务员考试网上市场中处于领先地位。2022 年，粉笔实现营业收入达 28.1 亿元，毛利润为 13.7 亿元，较 2021 年的 8.4 亿元同比增长 62.4%，同期毛利率由 24.5% 提升至 48.6%，增长迅猛。

2. 粉笔的迭代与更新

粉笔认为教育本身需要迭代更新，特别是销售后期服务。为了保持产品的竞争力，粉笔从以下几个方面持续创新。

（1）员工的迭代

粉笔让强调个人主义的名师融入团队，提高了名师的团队合作能力。粉笔在招聘基础职位时也不会马虎，如招的客服人员一般都是应届毕业生。粉笔不仅为新人提供业务技能培训，还为员工提供独立思考的空间。粉笔要求客服部门每年都要总结一年内学员反馈的问题和解决方案。

（2）产品更新

目前，粉笔的讲义已经形成了很高的产品壁垒。产品更新中最重要的就是App的更新，如用户可以将自己申请的职位列表导入平台查看排名。

（3）服务升级

粉笔从最初收取学费并向用户发送讲义，演变成用户进入课程群，班主任将考试资料发到交流群。为了提高用户的积极性，粉笔采取了一系列措施，如进群前的知识评测、无聊的文字资料的音视频化等。

基于用户的反馈，粉笔持续完成自身的迭代更新，为学员提供细致周到的服务。粉笔把推广费用都投入到产品研发上，服务核心用户，因此深受用户好评。2018年，公务员国考报考人数创历史新高，但录取率逐年下降，竞争更加激烈，公考培训市场前景广阔。考生选择线上公考培训，一方面可以保护个人隐私，另一方面可以节省通勤时间。特别是在三四线城市备考的考生，这一庞大的人群更是被线下公考培训机构所遗忘。粉笔可以满足这部分考生的需求。

粉笔通过题库和智能修改系统，以免费学习资料吸引流量、打造品牌，然后通过线上直播教学、图书销售和线下面试课等方式完成变现。粉笔对试题进行深入研究，利用人工智能评估用户的学习水平，并以此为基础提供个性化试题，为用户一对一答疑。粉笔积极收集用户反馈，更新题库，并邀请名师加入团队，提供专业的试题分析。同时粉笔还模拟真题测试环境、增加答卷时限、智能批改，让用户身临其境。此外，粉笔还提供题库、教材、视频等学习资料，推送标准化课程和内容，完成渠道化转型。

虽然粉笔的利润不高，但是保持在相对合理的水平。粉笔持续增加内容、产品和服务，如软件版本每年更新20多次，后台服务等也在不断优化。这些都让粉笔逐渐发展成为在线公考培训市场的领导者。

3. 激烈竞争下的战略抉择

在线公考培训市场的巨大诱惑吸引了众多模仿者的出现。粉笔的系统班售价680元，模仿者售价590元，但低价竞争的模仿者随着时间的推移逐渐消失。

在线公考培训机构并不是粉笔真正的竞争对手，他们真正的竞争对手是盗版。对此，粉笔增加了讲义和练习册、提供在线问答、课程播放次数无限制且速度可以变化等。粉笔通过对自身产品的优化，不断提升产品壁垒。

随着在线教育直播的兴起，中公、华图的在线平台注册用户大幅增长。华图甚至还投资了一家在线公考培训机构，持股30%。2018年，中公借壳A股上市。华图教育以H股形式在中国香港主板上市，募集资金的60%用于实体业务拓展和网络建设。

粉笔在培训行业的成功，离不开互联网、人工智能和大数据。然而，这些技术在为粉笔带来巨大收益的同时，也很容易被竞争对手模仿。关于如何制定竞争战略，粉笔核心团队进行了激烈的讨论。有高管认为，粉笔的快速崛起表明，聚焦核心产品和核心用户是一条经得起市场考验的、切实可行的路线。虽然有竞争对手，但粉笔只要坚持现有的模式，也可以与竞争对手一起扩大优势。在未来几年，公考培训市场将保持稳定上升趋势。聚焦核心产品、持续优化服务的战略，不仅能让粉笔保持稳定增长，还能规避诸多风险。另一部分高管认为，粉笔与线下公考培训机构相比，优势在于平台化，企业只有发挥自身优势，才能永远立于不败之地。虽然粉笔取得了相当的成功，但公考培训在整个培训市场中只是相对较小的领域，故步自封只会让企业错失发展机遇。如果粉笔保留现有的经营模式，脱离公考培训的舒适区，将业务重点从公考扩展到其他职业考试，以谋求企业整体发展，这将是一个长远的规划。但是，放弃安全的路线，冲进一个相对陌生的领域，也会给粉笔带来很大的风险。

【案例5】

案例问题：

1. 与其他公考培训机构相比，粉笔公考在内部资源和能力方面有哪些优势？

2. 粉笔采取了什么竞争战略成功并迅速占领在线公考培训市场？采取这种战略的原因是什么？

3. 你认为未来公考培训市场有哪些机会和威胁？

4. 面对激烈的市场竞争，下一步粉笔应该采用哪种战略？

分析提示：

1. 企业的内部资源和能力能帮助企业获得竞争优势。本题可以从价值链的角度来分析和发现粉笔公考的内部核心资源和能力。例如，系统班的研发、App 的研发、人工智能评价、智能批改等都体现粉笔的研发能力；进群前的知识评测、文字资料的音视频化、软件版本每年更新 20 多次，后台服务等的不断优化等。

2. 波特提出了三种基本竞争战略：成本领先战略、差异化战略和集中化战略。成本领先战略是通过采取一整套行动，以低于竞争对手的成本，为顾客提供可接受的、具有某种特性的产品或服务。差异化战略是指以顾客认为重要的差异化方式来生产产品或提供服务的一系列行动。集中化战略是主攻某个特定的客户群、某产品系列的一个细分区段或某一个地区市场。可以根据粉笔的客户特点、产品内容等来分析其采用的是哪种竞争战略。

3. 这题考察企业的外部环境分析，结合案例中对竞争态势的描述，从宏观环境、产业环境和竞争环境的角度，识别企业外部环境中的机会与威胁。

4. 案例中给出了两种思路：一种是继续专注在公考培训业务上，另一种则是扩展到其他职业考试领域。可以从聚焦战略的优势和劣势的角度进行分析，也可以在内外部环境分析的基础上，运用 SWOT 分析法（优势 strength，弱势 weakness，机会 opportunity，威胁 threat）的分析工具，并给出战略决策建议。

案例来源：

1. 帅梦晨. 粉笔公考在线教育平台的竞争环境及策略研究. 2017.
2. 贺俊，刘艺，严学文. 粉笔公考的竞争战略. 2019.

案例 6

三家企业在甲醇钠产品上的动态竞争较量

知识点：

竞争对手分析、动态竞争、察觉－动机－能力（awareness-motivation-capability，AMC）模型

案例目的：

本案例通过介绍三家企业关于甲醇钠产品在多个市场上的竞争互动行为，帮助学生理解 AMC 模型的应用和动态竞争背后的逻辑。

案例正文：

1. 甲醇钠产品的经营情况

宁波浙铁江宁化工有限公司（以下简称江宁化工）成立于 2007 年 6 月，注册资金 7 亿元，隶属于浙江省交通投资集团有限公司，属于宁波市高新技术企业。公司主营化工产品的开发、生产、销售和技术服务，主导产品为顺酐和甲醇钠，产品销售网络覆盖全国多个省市，出口市场以欧美、东南亚为主。

安徽金邦医药化工有限公司（以下简称安徽金邦）创办于 1995 年，2001 年公司改制为民营企业，省级"重合同、守信用企业"，AAA 级银行资信，拥有自营进出口权。安徽金邦致力于精细化学品、医药中间体、生化试剂以及食品添加剂的开发与生产，主导产品有甲醇钠（粉末和溶液）、乙醚、乙醇钠（粉末和溶液），叔丁醇钠等。目前，安徽金邦已成为有实力的甲醇钠生产企业。安徽金邦高度重视产品质量和服务质量的提高，努力将技术与各方面的资源有效地结合在一起，不断改进产品的工艺和品质，较大限度地满足用户多方面的需求。公司通过了 ISO 9001 质量体系等一系列认证。安徽金邦的产品深受国内外用户的信赖，享有较高的声誉，国内市场占有率逐年上升，连续多年出口欧亚美洲许多国家和地区。

河南盛宏丰化工有限公司（以下简称河南盛宏丰）成立于 2012 年，厂区位于国

家级精细化工产业集聚区，占地6万平方米，年产16万吨甲醇钠。河南盛宏丰是一家集科研、生产、销售于一体的综合性化工企业，公司现有液体甲醇钠装置6套，年产21万吨液体甲醇钠和甲醇；固体甲醇钠装置两套，年产高纯固体甲醇钠2万吨。

这三家企业甲醇钠产品的市场范围接近，均分布在中国的浙江、江西、江苏、福建等省以及东南亚国家。从实力上来看，安徽金邦注册资金3000万元，入行业时间长，是行业标准的制定者，甲醇钠的质量及服务声誉均很好。河南盛宏丰注册资金1000万元，是亚洲最大的液体甲醇钠生产企业，市场遍布国内外。江宁化工是国家级高新技术企业，拥有宁波市级工程技术中心，增长势头强劲。从港口资源上来看，安徽金邦靠近南京港，河南盛宏丰靠近连云港，江宁化工靠近宁波港。所以，三家企业在下游市场、公司资源、公司规模和实力上相当，属于直接的竞争对手。

2. 动态竞争态势分析

本案例对江宁化工在2010—2020年与安徽金邦和河南盛宏丰展开的一系列的竞争行为进行梳理。三家企业这段时间经历了国内区域市场竞争、提高产品质量和改变状态来竞争、战略转移市场、国外市场开展竞争等诸多活动，竞争过程中各家企业纷纷展现了自身资源和能力的优势，过程值得研究和探讨。下面对这段时间内三家企业的各类竞争行为进行标记。

（1）进攻行为

为了在市场竞争中获得持续优势，企业通常会利用自身优势主动发起进攻行为。根据察觉、动机、能力这三种驱动力因素的不同程度，进攻行为可以被划分为六种类型：察觉（敏锐）、察觉（迟钝）、动机（强）、动机（弱）、能力（高）、能力（低）。察觉（敏锐）的进攻策略包括发布具有竞争冲击的广告、执行降价计划并广泛宣传、公开声明增长目标等；察觉（迟钝）的进攻策略一般从内部改善，如提高产品和服务质量、改进运营效率、结构合并重组等。动机（强）的进攻策略带有明显的侵略意识，并利用自有的资源优势冲击对手的核心或主要市场，或直接进攻并抢占巨大潜力和发展空间的市场；动机（弱）的进攻策略侧重共享，以进攻非核心的市场或在对手已经建立强势且稳固的市场地位的区域寻求一席之地。能力（高）

的进攻策略要求掌握对手难获得的专有技术或资源、必要时与外部参与者联合行动、同时企业内部各职能部门之间需要较为完善的协同机制支持等，能力（低）的进攻策略有降价、广告战、促销等。

（2）反应行为

应对进攻的反应行为一般分为四类：忽视、接纳、放弃和报复。当竞争者威胁不够，企业会选择忽视，不采取任何行动。当企业只占据市场容量的一部分，或增加竞争者反而能拓宽市场需求的总体规模，或是竞争行为将导致双方利益均出现不同程度受损时，企业会选择接纳竞争者的进入。放弃反应一般是由于企业无法抵抗竞争者的进攻，放弃市场反而会降低损失。报复反应要求实施主体具有或未来具有一定的竞争优势，通过自身的优势迫使竞争者不得不采用更强有力的市场拓展方式，从而防止竞争者出现或进一步出现侵犯行为。

3. 动态竞争过程和分析

表 6-1 所示为根据 AMC 模型梳理出的三家企业 2010—2020 年的动态竞争过程。

表 6-1　根据 AMC 模型梳理出的三家企业 2010—2020 的动态竞争过程

碰撞阶段	进攻者行动	反应者行动（AMC 模型）				反应行为选择	进攻行为结果
		反应者	察觉	动机	能力		
第一阶段	江宁化工扩建甲醇钠生产装置，大量产品低价进入市场	安徽金邦	安徽金邦了解江宁化工企业运营模式和营销策略	生产成本较江宁化工高，开拓其他领域市场，躲避恶性竞争	拥有丰富的客户资源，可以筛选出优质客户	接纳	成功进入浙江、江西、安徽、江苏等市场，浙江市场占据 40% 左右的份额
	安徽金邦增加固体甲醇钠生产负荷，拓展利润较大的高端医药市场	江宁化工	了解固体甲醇钠生产工艺以及投资等信息	固体甲醇钠生产技术要求较高，暂时精力不足	固体甲醇钠生产技术不熟悉	忽视	基本占领华东地区固体甲醇钠的市场
	江宁化工进行技术改造、提高产量、降低生产成本、提升产品品质	安徽金邦	关注江宁化工扩产计划以及销售区域和主要下游行业	降价销售，打压江宁化工，保持优势区域的市场占有率	产品结构、包装多样化、销售渠道广	报复	成功抢夺了安徽金邦的浙江、江西、福建等市场的部分客户

续表

碰撞阶段	进攻者行动	反应者行动（AMC 模型）				反应行为选择	进攻行为结果
		反应者	察觉	动机	能力		
	安徽金邦扩张海外市场	江宁化工	江宁化工注重周边区域销售，对海外市场不敏感	产销基本平衡，无心拓展额外市场	进入市场不久，营销团队能力不足	放弃	成功扩张了海外市场，取得了丰厚的客户资源和利润
	安徽金邦提高产品质量，牵头制定行标	江宁化工	关注行标制定牵头企业的资质和标准	抢夺行标牵头制定名额，树立品牌形象	其他产品有牵头制定国标和行标的经验	报复	成功牵头制定2014版行标，树立品牌形象
	安徽金邦保留国内高利润的核心客户，大步进军东南亚市场	江宁化工	对海外市场不敏感	开发海外市场成本高，国内利润尚可	产量不足，无法开拓海外市场	放弃	出口量大幅提升，获取了高额利润
	江宁化工技改扩产，填补区域市场空缺	安徽金邦	对国内低价、竞争激烈市场兴趣不大	海外生物柴油市场蓝海市场，利润较高	无富余产品内销竞争	忽略	进一步提高了周边市场占有率
第二阶段	河南盛宏丰大量扩大产能，填补国内周边市场空缺，并迅速进入成长较快的东南亚生物柴油市场	江宁化工	对海外市场不敏感	开发海外市场成本高，国内利润尚可	产销平衡，无心开拓海外市场	放弃	成功开拓了东南亚生物柴油市场
		安徽金邦	了解河南盛宏丰出口的港口、价格、客户等资料	降价销售，保持东南亚市场的占有率	东南亚市场知名度高，业务流程熟悉	报复	
	安徽金邦放弃国内部分市场，进一步提高海外市场份额	江宁化工	对海外市场不敏感	开发海外市场成本高，国内利润尚可	产销平衡，无心开拓海外市场	放弃	降低了河南盛宏丰在东南亚生物柴油市场的占有率
		河南盛宏丰	关注下游客户反馈信息和海关出口数据	降价销售，联合出口中间商，开拓出口渠道	产能充足，成本优势较大，不惧价格战	报复	
	江宁化工周边市场萎缩速度加快，开拓海外市场	河南盛宏丰	关注下游客户反馈信息和海关出口数据	降价销售，保持东南亚市场占有率	国外市场有一定知名度，成本优势较大	报复	成功进入了东南亚市场，但占有率很低
		安徽金邦	关注下游客户反馈信息和海关出口数据	保持一定的东南亚市场占有率，多余产能转做固体产品销售给高端医药客户，获取相对较高的利润	国外市场知名度较高，客户关系良好，产品结构多样化，销售渠道较宽	接纳	

续表

碰撞阶段	进攻者行动	反应者行动（AMC 模型）				反应行为选择	进攻行为结果
		反应者	察觉	动机	能力		
	江宁化工搬迁、扩产，生产成本进一步下降，提高对东南亚及周边市场的出口量，提高海外市场占比	河南盛宏丰	预测江宁化工进入销售区域时间和价格	积极备战，准备降价	成本低，客户关系良好，市场竞争能力强	报复	提高了东南亚市场的占有率
		安徽金邦	预测江宁化工进入销售区域时间和价格	积极备战，准备降价	生产和运输成本高，正面竞争能力不足	报复	
	河南盛宏丰扩产，向国内外已有份额的市场进攻，同时设计固体甲醇钠生产装置，进军高端医药市场	安徽金邦	预测河南盛宏丰销售区域、时间和价格	准备接受价格战	市场经营时间较长，客户信任度高	报复	侵占安徽金邦和江宁化工国内外部分市场，布局了国内高端医药市场
		江宁化工	预测河南盛宏丰销售区域、时间和价格	准备接受价格战	国内区域液体部分市场存优势，靠近宁波港口出口成本低	报复/部分接纳	
	安徽金邦拓展南美、非洲等海外市场	江宁化工	江宁化工密切关注南美、非洲等其他海外市场，寻找合适时机进入	拓展海外客户群，获取较高的利润	出口部门积累了出口经验，靠近宁波港口运输成本低	接纳	扩大了南美和非洲市场，缓解销售压力
		河南盛宏丰	河南盛宏丰重心在于快速发展的东南亚生物柴油市场，对其他区域市场不敏感	东南亚生物柴油市场发展较快，必须牢牢把控	开发新市场能力不足	忽视	
	河南盛宏丰再次扩产，增加国内外市场占有率，争做亚洲产能龙头	安徽金邦	预测河南盛宏丰销售区域、时间和价格。了解河南盛宏丰扩产后的实际产能	降低外国生物柴油的市场占有率，将相应的销量去挤占河南盛宏丰在国内高端医药市场占有率。争抢做亚洲产能龙头，建设企业的产品品牌	国外市场存较大影响力，国内市场知名度较高，高端市场提高占比较易	报复	提高了国外生物柴油市场的占有率，暂坐了亚洲产能龙头的位置，提高了企业及其产品的知名度
		江宁化工	预测河南盛宏丰销售区域、时间和价格	准备接受价格战	生产消耗成本占据优势，又靠近宁波港口出口成本低	报复	

续表

碰撞阶段	进攻者行动	反应者行动（AMC 模型）				反应行为选择	进攻行为结果
		反应者	察觉	动机	能力		
江宁化工重新布局市场，开发周边的高端医药市场		安徽金邦	关注江宁化工何时进入高端医药市场	利用前期积累的品牌优势，抢夺优质客户，保持市场占有率	市场进入早，忠实客户多，品牌形象良好	报复	成功进入周边的高端医药市场，并占领了一定市场份额
		河南盛宏丰	关注江宁化工何时进入高端医药市场	准备接受价格战	生产总体成本低，价格存一定优势，产能龙头知名度较高	报复	
安徽金邦进一步扩产，对生物柴油和国内大众市场展竞争，夺回亚洲产能龙头地位		江宁化工	预测安徽金邦进入市场的时间和价格	准备接受价格战	生产成本和出口成本低，产品质量好、口碑优良	报复	提高了生物柴油市场的占有率，并成功夺回亚洲产能龙头的地位
		河南盛宏丰	预测安徽金邦进入市场的时间和价格，了解安徽金邦产能新增的数量	准备接受价格战，同时做好充足准备来应对安徽金邦抢夺亚洲产能龙头地位	生产总体成本低，价格优势大，国内外市场已有较大知名度	报复	

通过对竞争过程的描述，可以看出安徽金邦进攻质量高、能力强，特别是善于开拓新市场和新领域，但从反击频率不如河南盛宏丰，在激烈竞争的大众市场反击力度不强。河南盛宏丰虽然进入市场较晚，但进入市场后连续发起猛烈的进攻和反击，市场领域及份额上升速度较快，但是进攻质量和反击能力不如安徽金邦。江宁化工在2018年之前进攻和反击能力较弱，2018年之后进攻手段开始多样化，进攻能力变强。同时表6-1也表现出，安徽金邦采取了差异化竞争战略，在销售市场上属于开拓者。安徽金邦利用自身入行以来积累的资源，不断提高产品品质形成优质品牌，与竞争对手形成差异化，在市场端不断开拓新空间，不与国内其他竞争对手直接竞争，从而获取高额利润。安徽金邦的劣势是新市场开发成本和销售投入极高。河南盛宏丰执行成本优势战略，不断利用自身产品结构的成本优势提高市场占有率，一步一步将销售市场做大，这样能促进产业和产能的扩张，进一步降低成本，形成良性循环。但其劣势也较为明显，对培养生产力量过于执着，销售端能力较差，产

品品质和品牌形象较差，大多数情况下是以低于市场平均价来获得高额的市场份额，结果是确实明显提高了市场占有率，但获利不佳。

案例问题：

1. AMC 模型的三个主要因素在案例中是如何体现的？
2. 结合案例分析三家企业在动态竞争中的进攻行为和反应行为有哪些差异？
3. 结合案例分析三家企业在动态竞争中的竞争战略有哪些差异？
4. 根据案例中所描述的动态竞争过程，你会为这三家企业提出哪些竞争建议？

分析提示：

1. AMC 模型是研究、分析和建立了竞争者之间采取进攻行为和受到攻击后是否回应的预测模型，并将核心驱动因子归结为其他企业行动的觉察、自身回应的动机和自身回应的能力三方面。三个主要因素的内涵可以从微观、宏观两个层面进行解读。

2. 基于 AMC 模型三种驱动力因素的不同程度，不同的进攻行为可以被划分为六种类型，分别为察觉（敏锐）、察觉（迟钝）、动机（强）、动机（弱）、能力（高）、能力（低）。反应行为分为四类，分别是忽视、接纳、放弃和报复。可以从三家企业的多次进攻和反应行为中观察差异。

3. 可以根据三家企业动态竞争行为，结合差异化战略、成本领先战略的特点来判断其所采用的竞争战略。差异化战略主要体现在产品、服务的差异化上，成本领先战略意味着企业提供质量过得去的产品，但成本比竞争对手更低廉。

4. 分析竞争过程中三家企业的察觉、动机和能力情况，对比三家企业在资源和能力上的优势和劣势，给出战略建议，可以坚持原有战略或者提出新的战略。

案例来源：

本案例是编者根据企业调研及网上公开数据整理改编而得。

案例 7

多元化：红帮裁缝的岔路口

知识点：

战略管理的重要性、公司层战略、多元化战略

案例目的：

本案例介绍了宁波服装企业的多元化历程，着重梳理杉杉和雅戈尔截然不同的战略路径，以帮助学生理解战略管理的重要性，了解多元化战略的相关概念，理解多元化作为一种战略手段，并没有优劣之分，关键是多元化的管理过程。

案例正文：

宁波人做西式服装由来已久。清末民初，一些欧洲人通过宁波口岸到中国经商，就找当地人做服装。由于这些欧洲人都长着红胡子，衣服样式也与当地人大不相同，所以管这些给这些外国人做衣服的宁波人叫作"红帮裁缝"。在中国服装史上，"红帮裁缝"创下了五个第一：第一套西装、第一套中山装、第一家西服店、第一部西服理论专著和第一家西服工艺学校。而宁波，拥有众多的国内一线服装品牌，包括杉杉、雅戈尔、罗蒙、太平鸟、唐狮、培罗成等。其中，李如成的雅戈尔和郑永刚的杉杉名气最响。

向左走，向右走？

同为国内服装业的领头羊，雅戈尔和杉杉却走出了不一样的产业延伸道路。服装面料的好坏和采购，直接影响到服装的质地、生产制造流程，以及对消费者需求的反应速度。2002年，雅戈尔与日本伊藤忠和日清纺合资兴建纺织城，开始进军产业链上游。依据服装面料优势，雅戈尔推出了耐久免熨纯棉衬衫，受到市场热捧，现已成为公司主打的衬衫产品。此外，为应对国际服装市场对纺织面料在环保和舒适度上的高要求，雅戈尔联合中国人民解放军总后勤部军需装备研究所研发出改良育种的汉麻纤维，汉麻产品具有柔软透气、防霉除臭等功效。2007年，雅戈尔投资

西双版纳雅戈尔实业有限公司（原汉麻产业投资控股有限公司）。2009年，雅戈尔与宁波宜科科技实业股份有限公司联合投资的世界首条汉麻纤维生产线正式建成投产，年产5000吨的生产能力形成了原料供应保障。尽管汉麻产业目前仍处于亏损状态，但李如成坚信汉麻产品在医药、食品、保健品等领域的应用上巨具有大商机。2020年，雅戈尔营业收入达57.50亿元，利润总额达10.82亿元。

与雅戈尔不同，杉杉主要在产业下游发力，提出了"多品牌、国际化的战略"。杉杉与日本伊藤忠、意大利法拉奥、法国雷诺玛，以及法国高级时装公会等国际著名的服装企业与机构，建立了长久的合作关系。鼎盛时期的杉杉在全国拥有2000多家门店，国内西服市场占有率达37.4%，而在2018年缩减至1226家门店，市场占有率仅为1.55%。同年，杉杉将服装业务剥离出来，单独成立杉杉品牌运营股份有限公司。

多元化的"馅饼"

据一位服装业高管透露，"凭经验看，服装产业做到年产值5千万到1亿元的销售额时，服装的库存量增大，基本上就不赚钱了"。雅戈尔和杉杉开始放眼其他业务领域，迈开了多元化的步伐。

早在1992年，雅戈尔就已经拥有了第一家地产公司——雅戈尔置业控股有限公司（以下简称雅戈尔置业），但其房地产业务的高速发展是在2000年。2000年，雅戈尔置业启动"东湖花园"项目，在宁波地产界打响了"第一枪"。2002年，雅戈尔置业实现营业收入达5.34亿元，开始实施"长三角发展战略"，走出宁波，进军台州市场；2004年进入苏州市场，2007年相继进入杭州和绍兴市场。2010年，雅戈尔的地产业务收入达68.43亿元，首次超过服装业务收入，成为第一大主营业务。2020年，雅戈尔的地产业务收入达50.71亿元，利润总额为20.14亿元。在服装业受到新冠肺炎疫情的冲击时，地产业务对雅戈尔的业绩做出了突出贡献。作为多元化的重要支撑，雅戈尔也进入了金融投资领域。1997年，雅戈尔参股宁波银行。1999年，雅戈尔参股中信证券。雅戈尔进行一系列的股权投资，高峰时期持有上市公司股票市值高达240亿元。雅戈尔营业收入随着市场行情频繁波动，经历了两次金融危机的冲击，雅戈尔逐步缩减了金融投资业务。2019 年，按照新金融工具准则，雅戈尔 196 亿元的可供出售金融资产需要重新分类为"以公允价值计量且其变动计入当期损益的金融资产"。

在雅戈尔大举进军房地产行业之际，杉杉也以其服装主业造就了 100 个千万富翁，但账目盈利不多，库存居高不下。1998 年年底，杉杉总部迁入上海浦东，尽管错过了房地产的黄金十年，杉杉在科技领域的辛勤耕耘迎来了新能源产业发展的春天。

2020 年，杉杉的锂电池材料业务主营业务收入达 69.15 亿元，同比增长 1.83%，归属上市公司的净利润达 2.88 亿元。目前，杉杉已经成为全球规模最大的锂电子电池材料综合供应商，并在技术先进性和规模化方面跻身世界前 3 位，拥有 4 个国家 863 个科技项目的成果和数十项自主专利。此外，杉杉还通过投资宁波银行、徽商银行等金融机构获得投资回报，并涉足融资租赁、商业保理等类金融业务。杉杉已经由国内第一家上市的服装企业成功转型为新能源产业领军企业，成为集科技、时尚、金融服务、城市综合体和贸易物流等产业于一体的多元化企业集团。

专业化管控异曲同工

多元化本身并没有优劣之分，重点是多元化的管理。一般而言，多元化成功的关键在于通用性资源的支持和专业化管理。通用性资源包括管理、资金、品牌、技术、渠道等。雅戈尔和杉杉在前期经营中已经树立了良好的品牌形象，积累了较多的现金流，为扩展其他业务打下基础，加上与当地政府建立了良好的关系，这些独特性资源也为多元化的经营提供了重要支持。

在专业化管理中，雅戈尔和杉杉都奉行"专业的人做专业的事"。聘请职业经理人管理相应的产业公司，是企业管理多元化业务的重要手段，但会产生委托代理问题，对此杉杉和雅戈尔有不同的解决办法。杉杉的职业经理人经总部推荐，由董事会任命，总部将各产业公司的经营权充分下放，通过财务、内控、审计、绩效管控等对各产业公司进行垂直管理，每年进行两次内部管理分析评估和一次绩效审计。对产业公司经营团队的业绩考核以净资产回报率为核心，以增长和风险控制指标为辅助，充分激发他们的创造性、主动性和积极性。

雅戈尔也从外面寻找专门的职业经理人对相关产业进行管理。与此同时，李如成通过股权控制收紧对雅戈尔的管控权。截至2020年年底，李如成父女共占宁波盛达发展有限公司98.73%的股份，曲线增持雅戈尔。此次股权变更完毕后，李如成父女将直接、间接持有雅戈尔33.03%股权。

红帮裁缝的转型

像雅戈尔这样的服装企业，具有完整的生产链、庞大的国内市场销售渠道和强大的品牌号召力，但在电子商务时代受制于消费习惯的影响，服装库存激增，承受了巨大的压力。自2013年起，整个服装行业出现严重的供给问题，杉杉也陷入高库存的困境。2020年，杉杉服装库存金额高达4.3亿元，占总资产的48.7%。

在宁波，不仅仅是雅戈尔和杉杉选择多元化的道路，其他服装龙头企业也纷纷实施了多元化战略。例如，太平鸟进入了汽车贸易、家居用品和商业投资等领域，罗蒙也涉足房地产开发和国际贸易等领域。伴随着服装业务发展的现金流和库存量的与日俱增，多元化是企业在寻找市场机会与回避风险下的必然选择。

但我们也应当看到，服装除了承载着企业家的情感，作为百姓生活必需品，其巨大需求也是企业应对外部风险的重要保障。2019年，在雅戈尔成立40周年之际，雅戈尔实控人李如成高调宣布："回归服装主业。"这家从服装、房地产、投资等业务中获利颇丰的企业开始收缩业务范围。杉杉已成功转型为高科技企业，郑永刚曾对媒体坦言："靠服装赚钱的时代早已过去，我更希望大家称呼我为金融家。"

【案例7】

案例问题：

1. 结合案例谈谈什么是公司层战略？它为什么重要？
2. 案例中宁波服装企业选择多元化战略的主要原因是什么？
3. 雅戈尔和杉杉采用的是相关多元化战略还是无关多元化战略，为什么？
4. 如何评价雅戈尔和杉杉的多元化战略。

分析提示：

1. 公司层战略是解决当企业有多个业务时如何获取竞争优势的问题。案例中所举例的宁波服装企业都涉足多个业务领域，如何在这些业务间进行资源分配是公司总部需要思考的重要问题。

2. 可以从企业多元化的动因来分析这个问题。公司采用多元化战略的原因有很多，包括寻找利润空间更大的市场、规避风险、范围经济、产业链整合、提高市场影响力等。

3. 根据多元化战略的层次和各业务间的关联程度，多元化战略可以划分为不同的类型。根据多个业务之间能否共享资源，可以将多元化战略区分为相关多元化战略和无关多元化战略。

4. 多元化战略成功的影响因素包括多个业务之间能否产生协同效应、是否过度多元化、管理难度的增加是否可控、管理者多元化动机等。企业是否应该采用多元化战略，以及该采用哪种多元化战略需要权衡多元化战略可能带来的收益与风险。

案例来源：

本案例是编者根据网上公开数据整理改编而得。

案例 8

企业并购中的整合：
海信与科龙

知识点：

并购战略、整合、有效并购的影响因素、并购中的员工抵制

案例目的：

本案例介绍海信并购科龙的过程，强调整合在并购中的意义和价值，引导学生理解企业并购战略的理论内涵，以及影响有效并购的关键因素。

案例正文：

科龙被海信并购后，于2007年公司名更新为海信科龙电器股份有限公司（以下简称海信科龙）。随着公司发展壮大，为更好地反映其主营业务及战略定位，满足公司品牌管理与品牌发展的需要，2018年海信科龙将A股证券简称变更为"海信家电"。随之，公司中文全称由"海信科龙电器股份有限公司"变更成"海信家电集团股份有限公司"（以下简称海信家电集团）。经过历年发展，海信家电集团现已成为全球以家电制造为主的超大规模企业，经营范围包括开发、制造冰箱等家用电器，产品内、外销售和提供售后服务，运输自营产品。截至2021年9月，海信家电集团已具备年产冰箱1350万台、家用空调1800万台、中央空调360万台、洗衣机340万台、冷柜340万台，以及模具1700余套（其中大型塑料模具900余套，精密模具200余套，冲压模具600余套）、钣金加工20万吨以上的强大产能，产品销往全球130多个国家和地区。虽然从并购结果来看，当年被视为"蛇吞象"式的并购是非常成功的，但当年的并购过程并非一帆风顺。

2004年，海信旗下拥有彩电、空调、冰箱等多类产品，共计实现销售额273亿元。而当时的科龙，作为白色家电业的龙头企业，旗下拥有科龙、容声、康拜恩、华宝等冰箱及空调品牌，公司有在A股和H股进行上市，由格林柯尔集团公司控股。同年，科龙实现销售额84亿元。科龙2004年年报显示，科龙的冰箱业务获得全中

国冰箱的销量冠军，并在外销业务上取得了87.5%的增加率；而在空调市场，科龙稳居行业第4位。因此，如果成功并购科龙，海信将成为国内冰箱行业龙头，单从冰箱和空调两大行业来看，此次并购必将成为典型的"蛇吞象"式并购。

科龙最早是一家广东的乡镇企业，1984年始生产冰箱，是中国最早生产冰箱的企业之一，容声冰箱是其副牌。国产冰箱的标签加上优秀的质量以及品牌意识，让科龙冰箱一时成为市场的宠儿。但是科龙股权纠纷不清、挪用贪污问题严重，混乱的管理让科龙由盛转衰，亏空越来越多。2005年，科龙报出6000万元巨亏，截至当年8月31日，涉诉讼案件108件。随后，海信派人赴广东顺德实地了解情况，经过多次的考察、谈判以及政府相关部门的帮助，格林柯尔及海信最终在2005年9月9日签署了转让协议，双方同意初步拟定标的股份的转让价格为9亿元。

由于科龙出现了持续亏损，造成金融机构、供货商和经销商等对其信心不足，资金紧张，一度出现停产的状况。面对这种状况，海信在没有确定股权的情况下，提前介入科龙的企业经营，以避免其继续"失血"。为此，海信与科龙签署了科龙产品在中国市场全面销售代理协议，即海信作为科龙内销产品的独家代理，注入预付款购买科龙产品，负责向商家提供产品和货款回笼，在保全科龙原有销售体系的同时，协助科龙全面推广科龙产品。同时，海信派出包括总经理在内的30多名人员，占据科龙关键职位，对科龙进行全面托管。海信派出的人员中，既有高层管理者和中层管理者，也有相关的财务、管理、营销人员，全面掌握科龙的资金往来。

在科龙恢复生产的同时，海信对其组织结构进行了精简。科龙组织结构调整方案包括：科龙总部由原来的17个部门减少至12个部门，管理层级也由原来的6个减为3个；加强分公司总经理权力，实行总经理负责制；分别成立国内和国际两个营销总公司，且各自拥有独立的人事权和财务权；进一步强化定岗定编，撤销不必要的部门及职位。通过这些措施，科龙总部管理层仅剩下46人，配有7部公务用车和2名专职秘书。而在海信托管科龙之前，科龙总部管理层有近400人，配有27部公务用车和12名专职秘书。

此外，海信对科龙的日常管理也进行了调整。例如，托管前科龙下午的上班时间为 14：00，托管后科龙下午的上班时间调整到 13：30，下班时间也相应提前了半个小时，这使得员工工作效率明显提高。海信在科龙建立起严格的考勤制度，通过实行上下班打卡、签到等，改变了以往科龙一切凭部门领导监督或员工自觉的状况。托管后，科龙每月组织全国销售系统进行视频培训，和海信的销售管理人员一起开例会。例会内容包括：对上月经营情况进行分析；对当月市场销售进行规划；全面树立和强化科龙员工的经营意识。为加强管理，海信对科龙员工除了强调会议纪律，还严格监督纪律执行情况，甚至对漠视纪律者发出通告。

托管后，科龙的市场占有率得到了稳步回升。据中怡康市场研究机构统计，2005 年 11 月，科龙冰箱产品的市场占有率比 2005 年 7 月高出 2.53 个百分点，空调产品的市场占有率比 2005 年 8 月高出 1.62 个百分点。2005 年，科龙的海外销售也取得了令人满意的成绩：冰箱产品出口第四季度 3 个月均比 9 月增长 97% 以上；空调产品出口第四季度 3 个月分别比 9 月增长 33%、145% 和 483%。2006 年，科龙发布公告称，大股东广东格林柯尔企业发展有限公司已与青岛海信空调有限公司签订了股份转让补充协议，前者将所持有 26.43% 的科龙电器股份以 6.8 亿元价格转让给后者。至此，海信正式着手对科龙实行全面整合。

不过，海信与科龙在文化上的差异和碰撞似乎很难在短时间内消除。海信针对科龙展开的文化整合甚至被科龙员工视为吹毛求疵，科龙员工认为海信的企业管理过严。据科龙多年来公开披露的有关信息，在科龙多年的历史中，重要战略和人事决策及其成败，大股东及其代言人均是第一责任人。这些问题的存在使科龙高管对海信的并购整合充满了抵触情绪，随着海信管理人员的到位，科龙原高管陆续离去。

2008 年 2 月，临危受命进入科龙的海信"老臣"杨云铎出任海信科龙电器副董事长，在他的努力下，海信董事会通过了将海信冰箱和空调资产注入科龙的方案。2008 年 12 月，来自西门子的周小天出任海信科龙的第四任总裁。在周小天的带领下，科龙实现了平稳发展。2009 年，海信科龙以非公开发行 A 股股份的方式购买母公司青岛海信空调有限公司白色家电资产的方案获得证监会审核通过，并在 2010 年完成全部资产的交割。至此，海信科龙拥有了海信、科龙、容声三个"中国驰名商标"，并拥有了海信空调、海信冰箱、科龙空调、容声冰箱四个"中国名牌产品"，涵盖冰箱、空调、冷柜、洗衣机等多个领域。海信科龙的白色家电资产实现了整体上市。

截至2021年，海信科龙在产品的品类上发生了深刻的变革：从单一生产冰箱、空调的家电制造企业发展成为集生产冰箱、空调、洗衣机、厨房电器、环境电器、商用冷链等产品于一体的综合电器产品制造企业。

【案例8】

案例问题：

1. 海信并购、整合科龙的过程可以分为哪两个阶段？
2. 结合案例谈谈，企业并购后的整合有哪些内容？
3. 企业并购、整合中目标企业的员工抵制对并购绩效产生什么样的影响？
4. 结合案例谈谈，企业有效实施并购战略的关键因素有哪些？

分析提示：

1. 从科龙危机到海信托管，直至海信科龙实现其预期目标——利用上市公司整合色家白电业务，海信并购整合科龙的过程可以分为两个阶段，学生可从协议的执行过程进行分析。

2. 企业并购后的整合主要包括业务重组、财务重组和组织重组。业务重组是形成新的业务组合，形成新的地区业务分布。财务重组是形成新的资产与财务结构。组织重组是形成灵活、高效的组织体制。这三个内容相互影响、相互配合。

3. 员工抵制不会在整合调整时马上出现，而是在整合后的一段时间内随着整合的深入而逐渐增强。在对科龙并购整合的初期，海信派出高管整合科龙，但效果并不好。第四任总裁周小天从西门子离职，空降科龙，进行并购整合，绩效才得到提升。

4. 阻碍并购获得成功的因素主要有整合的困难、对并购对象评估不充分、巨额或非正常水平的债务、难以形成协同效应、过度多元化、管理者过度关注并购、规模过于庞大等。

案例来源:

1. 谢明磊.企业并购整合中的员工抵制:基于海信并购科龙的案例.山东社会科学,2012,(05):113-116.

2. 海信企业官网.

案例 9

海天：把产品覆盖到有海有天的地方

知识点：

国际化动机分析、国际化机会识别、国际化进入模式及其适合情境、国际化进入顺序、新兴经济体企业国际化

案例目的：

本案例以国内注塑机行业单项冠军示范企业海天的国际化过程为背景，重点分析在塑料机械市场竞争激烈的今天，中国注塑机企业如何跻身国际市场，进而理解企业在国际市场上是如何识别和利用机会的，以及如何解决困难的，最终帮助学生更好地理解国际化战略的实施与发展。

案例正文：

中国的注塑机是从最古老的人力手动注塑机，发展到液压手动、半自动、全自动，再到今天的全电动注塑机。海天国际控股有限公司（以下简称海天）在其中扮演了重要的角色。今天的中国市场，已经形成注塑机械年需求量约50亿美元的规模，其中包含国产设备、进口设备及外资厂设备投资的部分。国内注塑机械产值达到20亿美元的规模，其中海天已经成为国内乃至世界年产量第一的企业。

1966年，海天的前身江南农机厂机床厂成立。彼时，海天还只是个生产镰刀、锄头、水泵等农机工具的小作坊。后来，海天创始人张静章看到农民穿塑料鞋不易坏，便琢磨起塑料是怎么造出来的。1973年，海天第一台注塑机问世，并由此开启在注塑机行业一路"进击"的道路。1994年，海天注塑机产量已名列全国第一，并维持地位至今。但海天对自己和行业仍有着清醒的认识。张静章曾在媒体上表示，"尽管我们销售规模已经是全球第一了，但从技术角度来说，还不是第一。"通过更加积极的开放学习、全球研发协作，海天正朝着更广阔的空间迈去。

图 9-1 对海天的国际化进程按照时间顺序进行了梳理。海天于 2001 年率先在土耳其设立子公司，迈出了国际化的第一步；紧接着，2004 年海天进入巴西市场，将海外业务延伸至南美洲；2007 年以收购德国长飞亚为标志，海天首次进入欧洲市场，这是国际化的里程碑事件；从 2010 年开始，海天陆续进入越南、印度、印度尼西亚、墨西哥、泰国等新兴市场，相继成立海外子公司；2016 年，海天打入日本市场，并组建研发中心，在全电动技术方面实现了质的飞跃。

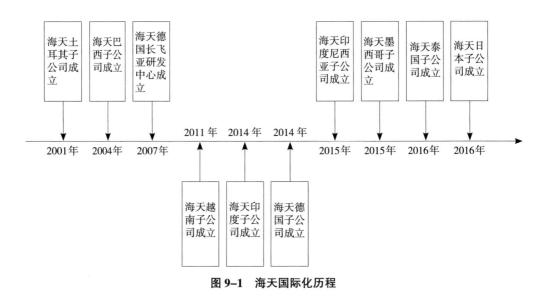

图 9-1　海天国际化历程

1. 试水土耳其

2001 年，海天在土耳其独资建立了海天土耳其子公司，因此拥有了第一家在海外的全资子公司，为当地客户提供销售及服务支持。海天之所以选择在土耳其建立第一家海外子公司，是因为土耳其处在亚欧板块的交界处，文化包容性高，来自亚洲的企业能够较快融入其中。张静章认为，就出口产品的最终市场而言，发现有些国家在复制中国的发展之路，比如土耳其。国外客户的需求与国内客户相似，于是海天一直将土耳其视为重要出口市场，也是海天"全球化战略"的重要一环。技术总监傅南红表示，土耳其子公司的建成为海天提供了全新的平台，全面提升了在当地的销售及服务水平。海天以土耳其子公司为中心，辐射周边国家和地区，从根本上解决了机电产品在国际上交货期晚和售后服务困难的问题。

通过在土耳其的尝试，海天牌注塑机已被外经贸部确认为"国家级重点支持和发展的名牌出口商品"，海外销量年年增长。海天2002年海外销售额为3500万美元，2003年海外销售额为5000万美元，2004年荣获"中国机械500强"称号，产品批量出口美国、欧洲、南美洲、中东、东南亚等50多个国家和地区，产量和销售额在中国居同行业首位。

而在海天的国际化战略中，土耳其市场的开拓仅仅是试水，海天有着更大的战略目标。一边是核心能力高超的欧洲劲敌，一边是消费水平不高的亚洲厂商，要如何找到一条过渡之路？

2. 巴西的本土化策略

2004年，海天在巴西独资建立了巴西子公司，主要进行生产、销售和服务工作。总部希望通过在巴西的发展能打开美洲市场。

海天巴西子公司当时缺少开展国际业务的人员，也没有海外投资的经验，但凭着一股冲劲，完成了"在当年建立、当年销售"这一极其困难的计划。海天巴西子公司坚持本土化，最初就只派了3个中国人去巴西，成立了巴西的管理团队。在现在看来明智的战略，在当时却遇到很多困难，如沟通和文化冲突等问题。海天认为，只有学习当地的制度和文化才能更好服务客户。从卖产品到卖服务，走服务型制造企业之路，是企业迈入产业链高端环节的必由之路。

3. 向德国学习

2001—2007年，海天都在为走进高端国际市场做准备。2005年，海天聘请德国塑机协会主席弗朗兹教授担任海天发展战略委员会委员，就公司的业务发展战略向董事会提供意见。2007年，海天收购德国长飞亚塑料机械制造有限公司，弗朗兹教授正式加入海天，担任执行副总裁，负责协调宁波研发部与德国长飞亚研发中心，共同开发全电动注塑机。通过共同努力，海天的电动注塑机取得了技术性突破，机器性能得到极大提升。2007年，海天成功开发出长飞亚天锐系列注塑机。

2014年，海天在德国建立了子公司。海天与德国公司合作是有历史渊源的。早在1995年，德国诺曼斯诺集团董事法郎兹到海天考察，3年后，双方合资成立德马格海天塑料机械有限公司，专做高端注塑机。德国的加工工艺、管理理念对海天日后的发展产生深远影响。

初步进入国际市场的海天面临着技术壁垒和生产需要的问题，海天一方面需要加快技术变革，另一方面又要同时兼顾国际市场的有序拓展。海天德国子公司总经理项林法说，向对手看齐最好的方式就是直面竞争对手，只有深入德国才能快速发展，初步定下了海天要去德国建立公司的想法。同时海天内控本部部长兼投资关系部总经理施华均表示，当时国内很多塑料制品价格昂贵，因为其设备依赖进口，企业开支大，海天看到大机器市场被国外垄断，就决定进军装备制造领域。竞争压力感知和增长的需要，提高服务能力，强化售前及售后服务等都是海天对德国厂房做出投资决定时考虑的因素。

2007 年正式进入德国之后，海天以全资办厂的形式陆续在印度、印度尼西亚、墨西哥、泰国建立了子公司，深入南亚、东南亚、北美洲的市场，大规模投资新兴经济体市场。

4. 做大印度市场

海天在印度成功建立子公司主要得益于印度塑料工业的发展环境。2008 年，印度销售的注塑机中约有 37% 来自进口，远高于 2002 年的 11%。而在进口的机器中，半数以上来自中国。2009 年起，印度政府及主管机构等帮助发展当地的注塑机行业。2014 年，海天已经做到产销量全球第一。

印度的注塑机行业下游产业发展旺盛，也非常欢迎来自中国的机器。海关在印度建立的新厂房具备成品机库存、零配件库存、试模中心和培训中心等功能，提供了更充裕的场地，扩充了生产能力，缩短了交货周期，为当地客户带来了高效、便捷的服务及支持，这大大提高了印度政府和市场对于海天的满意度。

5. 在墨西哥建工厂

2019 年 5 月 28 日，海天墨西哥子公司在墨西哥第二大城市瓜达拉哈拉市举行了新工厂奠基仪式。该工厂旨在实现海天注塑机产品的本地化生产与装配，主要用于满足墨西哥市场的需求，是海天的出口平台之一。海天执行董事张剑鸣先生表示，新工厂的建设是海天推进全球业务的重要战略布局之一，未来海天将在新工厂的基础上全面提升生产效率，通过技术创新、服务创新和管理创新，以更优质的产品和更便捷的服务持续为客户创造价值。这个新工厂也是墨西哥首个注塑机制造基地。墨西哥作为拉丁美洲第二大塑料消费市场，拥有巨大的市场需求和广阔的发展前景。从1999年开始，海天便在墨西哥市场开始了注塑机的销售与服务。截至2018年，海天在墨西哥市场的年销售额占中国所有出口注塑机总量的40%，海天已成为墨西哥塑料加工行业最受信赖的品牌之一。

6. 在日本建研发基地

海天能将公司开到国外，最大的原因还是自身技术的提高。从液压注塑机到全电动注塑机，海天为了追赶国际先进技术的脚步，在技术开发方面一直是铆足了劲。2016年，海天建立了日本子公司，进行技术研发和产品销售服务。这对海天追赶国际一流塑机技术来说，是很大的跳跃。在日本学习全电动节能机型的技术，对海天在全球的发展是十分关键的。

海天日本子公司的战略与其他子公司不同，目标不仅限于盈利增长点，更注重推动横向的行业发展。由于国内的注塑机行业竞争愈来愈激烈，海天在日本建立研发中心，既要学技术又要打入日本市场，以此来保护国内市场。2016年在日本成立的"海天华远日本机械株式会社"，进一步提升了海天在日本的销售和服务等级，可以为当地客户提供完善的售前和售后服务。海天在日本市场的发展起到了联动效应，促进全球战略布局实现新的突破。

海天在日本还积极与当地企业合作。例如，日本新泻机械科技与海天在日本成立了一家合资企业，专注于电动注塑机技术的发展，使日本新泻机械科技能够利用海天的大规模生产技术，在日本以较低的成本生产出高精度的日本造模机。海天整个链条依靠产业协同，需要提升品质。于是选择从电镀入手。2014年，海天学习日本的模式，着手自建电镀车间。海天不断研发投入，对标大型注塑机技术第一的奥地利恩格尔集团，向技术水平全面领先目标进军。

回顾海天国际化的历程，不难发现：海天进入国际市场是从海外销售开始的，采取代理制。经过多年努力，海天产品基本在海外市场站稳脚跟，但 2007 年之前仅限于中低端市场。收购德国长飞亚塑料机械制造有限公司之后，海天加快海外市场扩展，在日本等国家成立分公司、工厂和技术中心，发达国家成为海天出口的主要目标市场。

海天已建成完善的产品组合，实现了塑料加工产业链全覆盖。在国内业务受益于市场复苏和国外业务布局日臻完善的背景下，2018 年，海天推出三代注塑机，这种快速的产品更新迭代进一步巩固了海天的领先地位。

2020 年，海天发力高端市场，推行"小型吨位注塑机全电化，大型吨位注塑机二板化"战略，长飞亚电动等系列发展更为强劲，预计未来三年实现复合增速 30% 以上。截至 2020 年，海天已经在海外 9 个国家建立了子公司，在 60 多个国家都有了自己的代理，将产品出口至 130 个国家，国际化之路越走越远。2021 年，海天的注塑机销售额增长了 35.7%，达到创纪录的 160 亿元，交付机器超过 5.6 万台，在中国的销售额同比增长了 33%，海外的销售额则达到了 49.3 亿元，同比增长 40.1%，出口量首次突破 1 万台。海天在北美、东南亚、欧洲和南美的市场份额增加。海天的主要产品系列 Mars 全年销售额稳步攀升 33.2%，达到 17 亿美元。

海天计划以全球四个中心（中国、土耳其、巴西、德国）辐射周边国家和地区，要比肩欧洲注塑机，向高端市场发起挑战。

【案例 9】

案例问题：

1. 海天进入国际市场的主要原因是什么？

2. 海天主要采用了什么国际化战略？

3. 根据海天在海外开设子公司的路径，分析海天是以什么样的顺序进入其他国家，而形成这样的顺序的原因是什么？其中有何种规律？

4. 海天应该如何部署未来的全球化战略？

分析提示：

1. 该题考察的是企业国际化的动因，可以从国际化竞争、来源国劣势、动态能力等角度来思考。以国际化动机、机会识别、新兴经济体国际化为理论依据，分析在塑料机械市场竞争激烈的今天，中国的注塑机如何跻身国际市场。

2. 国际化战略主要包括全球化战略、多国化战略以及跨国战略等。

3. 该题可以从国际化动机、国际化机会识别等角度分析海天在发展过程中所面临的困难和机会，来展现出海天在不同情境下运用的进入模式等。由于核心技术封锁，加上服务费用高昂、国内专业维修人员稀缺，海天加快发展的脚步频频受阻，希望走出去，将品牌建设做得更好，于是开始了第一次海外建公司的经历，在土耳其开设了第一家海外子公司。海天积累了多年的海外经营经验之后，又在德国开设了子公司，这是在欧洲市场的一大突破，也是海天国际化进程的一大转折点。

4. 该题可以从结合企业所处的内外部环境，对海天今后开展国际化的市场选择、战略制订等提出建议。

案例来源：

本案例是编者根据企业调研及网上公开数据整理改编而得。

案例 10

京东的合作战略

知识点：

战略联盟、公司层战略联盟、业务层战略联盟、国际战略联盟

案例目的：

本案例通过介绍京东的合作战略，引导学生理解战略联盟的含义与类别，了解公司层战略联盟、业务层战略联盟及国际战略联盟的实例，思考不同类型战略联盟的差异与联系。

案例正文：

2014年，京东赴美国纳斯达克上市的准备工作进入最后冲刺的阶段。经过2012年大规模的品类扩张、2013年企业形象标识的全面更换，京东已经将自身打造为大型的综合性电商平台，第三方卖家比例不断提高。然而，面对一骑绝尘的淘宝与迅速扩张的天猫，京东的经营压力巨大，在主营业务持续亏损、销售费用与管理费用暴涨的情况下，如何进一步扩大流量入口、增加商品交易额度并提高利润率，就成为京东领导者时刻关注的核心问题。

1. 京东与腾讯的公司层合作

渴求流量入口的京东与互联网巨头腾讯寻找到了合作的点。对于京东来说，它迫切需要社交媒体所带来的巨额流量引入，而腾讯拥有微信和QQ两大移动端入口，用户基数巨大、黏性强，是不可多得的巨额流量门户。而对于腾讯来说，虽然接连投资了易迅网、QQ网购和拍拍网，但这些电商在发展线下物流与仓储业务时不得要领，而京东在物流与仓储建设方面则积累充足、经验丰富。如果双方能够合作，那么京东可以借助微信与QQ的广告推送产品信息，腾讯可以将自己并不擅长的电商业务转移给京东而将精力聚焦于更为擅长的游戏和媒体业务，还可以通过扶持京东而给予试图进入社交软件市场的阿里巴巴以有力反制。这样的合作，让腾讯在短

期具有收益，长期更具有战略价值；而让京东获得远超越亚马逊、易趣和当当的竞争优势，有力对抗强大的淘宝和天猫。

2014年3月，京东与腾讯宣布建立战略合作伙伴关系，京东向腾讯转让15%的股份以换取微信与QQ移动客户端的一级入口，同时获得QQ网购与拍拍网的所有股权、人员、资产，以及易迅网的少数股权。2014年5月，在京东登陆美国纳斯达克交易所成功上市时，腾讯依照承诺增持了5%的京东股份。在京东与腾讯达成合作协议后，京东2014年第四季度的移动订单出现了暴涨，同比增长372%，移动订单占京东所有订单的比例也提升至36%。

2015年10月，京东与腾讯宣布推出战略合作项目——"京腾计划"，双方将对接彼此的海量用户数据，打造名为品商的创新营销平台，即为品牌商家提供包括精准画像、多维场景、品质体验的全方位营销解决方案。一方面，京东掌握的数据可提供用户特征、行为偏好、广告偏好、购买偏好等方面的信息；另一方面，腾讯掌握的数据可提供人口特性、生活风格、兴趣爱好、使用环境等方面的信息。当腾讯的社交数据与京东的交易数据对接后，将能够更加清晰地把握客户特点并实现针对性的广告投放，从而有效完成精准营销。

2016年7月，腾讯与京东联合推出营销平台——"京腾魔方"。"京腾魔方"的主要思路是通过京东大数据，寻找到具备特定消费习惯的用户特征，并借助腾讯大数据寻找到满足特征的特定人群并进行精准广告推送。这样，用户将能够接收到自己所喜爱或需要的产品信息，而厂家也能够将产品准确传递给潜在顾客。2016年"双十一"期间，京东平台上的诸多知名品牌借助"京腾魔方"实现了用户规模和销量的倍增。而京东与腾讯也通过"京腾魔方"提供的营销服务获得了不菲的广告收益。

伴随着大数据技术的进步，在2018年4月所推出的新一代营销解决方案——"京腾魔方+"中，京东与腾讯将用户的数据进行整合，对用户的品牌偏好进行分析与预测。"京腾魔方+"能够进一步实现精细化的品牌营销，更精准地挖掘对特定品牌具有高度购买倾向的潜在顾客，将数字营销水平提升到了一个新的高度。京东与腾讯的合作能够成功，关键在于双方战略理念与目标的一致。在腾讯将社交平台、内容平台与京东的交易体系打通后，二者实现了零售行业线上线下跨场景的智慧连接，这不仅提升了消费者的消费体验，也为商家提供了有效的营销手段。这种深度合作的意义远远超出了单纯流量导入的价值。

2. 京东与互联网企业的业务层合作

在京东与腾讯通过合作重塑中国电商格局的同时，京东又与其他互联网企业进行了战略合作。2016年9月，京东与字节跳动宣布达成全面战略合作关系，并共同推出"京条计划"。"京条计划"主要涵盖三个方面：一是京东在今日头条 App 上开设一级购物入口"京东特卖"，借助京东电商开放平台，用户无须登陆京东商城就可以在今日头条 App 享受电商购物服务；二是基于今日头条的大数据能力，进行精准的广告投放；三是双方共同开展基于兴趣阅读的电商合作，通过导购、分佣等模式，帮助更多的头条号创作者变现。今日头条高达 5.5 亿的用户基数，为"京条计划"的成功奠定了基础。

2017年8月，京东与搜索引擎巨头百度联合推出了名为"京度计划"的战略合作框架。"京度计划"同样涵盖三个方面：一是京东在百度 App 内开设一级购物入口"京东特供"，同样与京东电商开放平台直接连接；二是百度将产品矩阵和用户群所产生的数据池，与京东的电商数据深度合作，帮助京东、京东的品牌合作伙伴、京东平台上的商家实现精准广告投放；三是通过导购、分佣等模式展开内容电商合作，提高内容变现能力。由于有百度领先的 AI 技术的支持，"京度计划"的精准度和响应速度都更具优势。

2018年4月，通过复制已经成熟的"京X"模式，京东又与奇虎360、网易、搜狗、爱奇艺、搜狐、新浪等互联网企业实现了战略合作。从业务关系来看，腾讯、字节跳动、百度、奇虎360、网易、搜狗、爱奇艺、搜狐和新浪等互联网企业，对京东来说就是媒体。通过与这些在细分领域均为第一大流量入口的互联网企业合作，京东得以覆盖几乎中国互联网100%的用户及用户场景。在这种情况下，入驻京东的品牌商只需要在系统内购买相关营销服务，就能够自动在各种互联网端口实现产品广告的全面覆盖和精准投放；而消费者无论通过何种接口购买商品，最后总会连接至商户的京东页面并通过京东高效的物流系统实现一站式交付。这样，京东构建的与互联网企业的合作平台，使得商户与客户能够直接相连，不受渠道、场景的限制，从而实现"无界零售"。

3. 京东与线下企业及国际企业的合作

在与线上互联网企业进行合作的同时，京东也在布局与线下企业的合作关系。

2015年8月，京东宣布以43.1亿元购买永辉超市10%的股票。京东入股永辉，目的就是强化京东最大的特色——垂直领域的自营程度，即采购、仓储、配送和售后一条龙。双方在协议中约定需强化联盟协同，定期开展高层沟通并商议合作重大事项，积极探索线上线下合作模式及线上到线下（O2O）业务发展，在仓储物流方面形成协作，共同挖掘互联网金融资源。而在入股永辉后，京东旗下的京东到家业务能够与永辉超市实现优势互补，提升彼此的竞争力。

2016年6月，京东宣布与国际零售业巨头沃尔玛达成深度战略合作，通过新发行并向沃尔玛转让市值15亿美元的京东普通股，京东获得了沃尔玛旗下的在线商城"1号店"的所有股权和资产。通过与沃尔玛的合作，京东能够借助沃尔玛在零售方面的资源优势强化京东在O2O领域的业务布局，并可以借助沃尔玛的海外资源实现京东的全球化战略，强化供应链及商超类产品的价格优势。此外，通过收购在华东地区市场具有影响力的"1号店"，京东不仅弥补了在该地区的市场短板，还获得了急需的超市品类资源，从而能够有效抵挡天猫超市与苏宁的进攻。

2017年6月，京东宣布出资3.97亿美元投资英国时尚购物平台发发奇，开始进军奢侈品市场。京东认为，发发奇的奢侈品渠道独一无二，这能吸引许多中国顾客。京东不会干涉发发奇的独立发展，但会在营销、物流与支付等技术层面为发发奇开展中国业务提供有力支持。

2017年12月，京东、腾讯与唯品会签署了战略合作协议，并分别认购唯品会5.5%、7%的股权。根据协议，唯品会将在微信钱包及京东平台获得入口。唯品会的优势业务集中于女性服饰、美妆和母婴产品，而京东的最大优势在于数码家电，二者的联手将实现用户与产品品类的互补。此后，京东进一步与唯品会在海外仓与供应链方面展开了深度合作，唯品会向京东开放 12 个海外仓资源，为京东全球购业务提供优质的海外仓储物流服务，而京东向唯品会开放近千条海外运输链路资源。

2018 年 6 月，谷歌宣布以 5.5 亿美元投资京东，并指出双方将开展战略合作项目，在全球多个地区合作开发零售解决方案，并探索打造下一代零售的基础设施，包括无人商店、无人货架、智能物流设备等。作为双方合作的试水，京东优选了一系列高品质商品，通过谷歌旗下电商在全球多个地区进行销售。借助与谷歌的合作，京东能更好地在全球进行业务扩张。京东期望能够进入欧洲市场与亚马逊竞争，而与谷歌的合作有效地促成这一计划的实现。

4. 结语

通过与其他企业的合作，京东在竞争白热化的电子商务市场站稳了脚跟，在巩固自有物流体系作为核心竞争优势的同时，弥补了自身短板，实现了优势互补和多赢。2019 年，京东的净营收接近 5800 亿元，同比增长近 25%，商品交易总额首次超过 2 万亿元。2021 年，京东集团全年营收创纪录地达到 9515 亿元，超越阿里巴巴 2343 亿元。在赶超阿里巴巴的过程中成长起来的京东，走出了一条行之有效的合作发展之路。

案例问题：

1. 结合案例回想，战略联盟有哪几种形式？京东的不同合作战略分别对应着哪一种形式？
2. 结合案例分析，京东的哪些战略联盟属于业务层战略联盟，其目标是什么？
3. 结合案例分析，京东的哪些战略联盟属于公司层战略联盟，其目标是什么？
4. 结合案例分析，京东的哪些战略联盟属于国际战略联盟，其目标是什么？

分析提示：

1. 战略联盟的主要实现途径有三种：合资企业、产权战略联盟与非产权战略联盟。学生可以结合正文中所描述的战略联盟的股权安排情况、联盟企业情况等来判断京东所选择的战略联盟方式。

2. 业务层战略联盟是用于提升在某一既定业务领域中核心竞争力的合作战略，有助于企业在单一业务领域获得成功。业务层战略联盟主要有互补型战略联盟、竞争反应型战略联盟、不确定降低型战略联盟。显性和隐形共谋会降低竞争强度、降低社会福利，因而违背了市场原则，一般不称作战略联盟。学生可以结合正文中那些仅在某一既定业务领域中提升竞争力的合作对业务层战略联盟进行判断。

3. 公司层战略联盟是为了扩大经营范围或提升跨业务的核心竞争力而采取的合作战略。其中，多元化战略联盟指通过共享资源实现多元化的战略联盟；协同战略联盟指通过共享资源来创造范围经济、实现协同效应的战略联盟；特许经营是指授权方将商标或经营方式授予被授权方使用并获得特许经营费和提成费的合作模式。学生可以结合正文中的合作战略是否实现了多元化、创造了协同效应或者通过授权品牌与商标的方式进行合作对公司层战略联盟进行判断。

4. 国际战略联盟是与外国企业资源共享来创造竞争优势的战略联盟。学生可以结合正文中的合作是否跨越了国界对国际战略联盟进行判断。

案例来源：

1. 张宸璐，李纯青，张洁，等. 风起云涌浪淘沙，志同道合方为谋：京东的战略联盟之路. 中国管理案例共享中心案例.

2. 李纯青，张宸璐，黄红丽，等. 桃园 N 结义：京东的品牌联盟之路. 中国管理案例共享中心案例.

案例 11

万科的公司治理之路

知识点：

所有权集中、管理层薪酬、董事会、公司控制权市场、防御策略

案例目的：

本案例通过介绍万科公司的公司治理特征与其所经历的几次公司治理事件，引导学生理解分散的股权结构对以职业经理人为主要特征的万科公司发展的影响，了解不同类型的薪酬激励计划的优势与劣势，领会在公司控制权市场中进攻与防御的交互性和复杂性。

案例正文：

万科企业股份有限公司（以下简称万科）成立于1984年，于1991年成为深交所第二家上市的公司。作为我国房地产企业的先驱和标杆，万科在发展过程中虽历经风雨，但总能持续蜕变，保持稳健的增长。在发展过程中，万科曾入选《福布斯》"亚洲最优50大上市公司"排行榜，多次获得国际权威媒体评出的最佳公司治理、最佳投资者关系等奖项，成为《财富》公布的"最受赞赏的中国公司"。根据《中国房地产企业百强研究报告》，万科始终位居中国房地产企业综合实力前三强，并于2006—2016年连续蝉联中国房地产企业综合实力冠军。

作为一家由创始人管理团队所主导、以职业经理人制度为核心的民营股份制企业，万科的管理制度先进健全、治理结构规范透明，长期以来受到各界的认可。然而，作为一家代表性企业，万科同样经历了一系列具有代表性的公司治理事件，而这一切都与万科独特的股权结构密切相关。与大多数国内上市公司高度集中的股权结构不同，万科的股权结构呈现相对分散的特征。1991—1999年，万科的最大股东是国企深圳新一代实业有限公司（以下简称新一代）及其母公司深圳市特发有限公司（以下简称深特发），其持有6%～9%的万科股份，且为唯一持股超过5%的股

东。2000—2015年，万科的第一大股东为华润股份有限公司（以下简称华润），持股比例始终保持在12%～15%。与此同时，鉴于万科管理层，特别是创始人王石和郁亮在业界的卓越影响力，无论是新一代、深特发还是华润，大股东长期以来对于万科管理层的自主决策始终是支持与默许的。这种创始管理团队主导—大股东默许—股权分散的公司治理特征，虽然使万科规避了在大多数中国企业中普遍存在的一股独大与内部人控制的弊病，却依然为万科带来了新的问题和挑战。

1. 有惊无险的"君万之争"

作为一次有惊无险的插曲，1994年的"君万之争"首次暴露了分散的股权结构所伴生的公司控制权隐患。1993年，由于业绩不如预期，万科股价低迷，一些中小股东对万科的经营产生了不满。1994年3月30日，万科的股票承销商君安证券（以下简称君安）宣布代表委托的四家股东——新一代（持股6.5%）、海南证券（持股1.1%）、香港俊山投资有限公司（持股1.7%）和创益投资有限公司（持股1.5%）召开新闻发布会，共同发起《改革倡议书》，指出万科的各种经营管理问题，并建议对万科的业务结构和管理层进行重组。发布会结束后，董事长王石紧急联系新一代的负责人，说服其退出与君安的结盟并发出声明。1994年3月31日，万科宣告停牌，使君安无法操纵股市。1994年4月1日，郁亮飞往海南岛，获得了海南证券的支持。1994年4月2日，万科发布公告，表明了新一代和海南证券对万科管理层的支持，而管理层对公司保持着稳定与强力的控制。1994年4月4日，万科股票复牌涨停，当日下午，万科召开新闻发布会，宣布"君万之争"结束。

"君万之争"没有动摇万科管理层对公司的实际控制，此后万科获得了快速发展。然而，良好的业绩却催生出了新的问题。由于万科的管理层并不大量拥有公司股份，伴随着公司发展而形成的规模庞大的中高层管理人员无法分享万科快速发展带来的战略收益，缺乏归属感。与此同时，万科的股东也担心管理层短视，迫切需要激励管理层以促使公司继续保持领先地位。因而，如何进一步设计股权结构、通过激励性薪酬设计来激发管理层的努力和创造力，就成为万科面临的新的公司治理问题。

2. 三次薪酬激励计划

为了解决内部激励问题，2006—2014 年，万科推行了三次薪酬激励计划。

2006—2008 年，万科实施第一次薪酬激励计划。这次薪酬激励计划采取的是限制性股票的方式。此计划面向所有中高层管理人员及业务骨干，通过设立激励基金，委托第三方在二级市场购买万科 A 股，在绩效条件满足后将股票作为奖励发放给相关人员。行权条件包括两个方面，业绩方面，当年的全面摊薄年净资产收益率需要超过 12%；股价方面，当年每股收益增长需超过 10%，且股价需要连年递增。然而，仅 2006 年达到了行权条件并实施了股票激励；2007 年，中国股市大跌，行权条件之一的股价指标未能达标；而 2008 年，受美国次贷危机影响，我国采取了紧缩银根的货币政策，房产交易额大幅下降，行权条件之一的业绩指标未能达标。由于设定的行权条件中包含员工无法掌控的外部因素，第一次薪酬激励计划并没有获得理想效果。

在第一次薪酬激励计划夭折后，许多骨干人员深受打击，公司士气不振。而且自 2010 年开始，房地产行业进入了新一轮调控，行业前景混沌不明。为了吸引并留住核心人才，2011—2013 年，万科决定进行第二次薪酬激励计划。万科的第二次薪酬激励计划采取的是股票期权的方式，即给予激励对象在未来一定期限内以预先确定的条件购买本公司一定数量股份的权利。此计划面向了中高层管理人员及核心业务人员，通过设置 1.1 亿份期权，鼓励员工在行权条件满足后，以低价购买公司股票并按照市价出售获利。吸取了第一次计划失败的教训，这一次的行权条件中仅包含业绩指标，要求 2011—2013 年的全面摊薄净资产收益率分别超过 14%、14.5%、15%。

相较于第一次薪酬激励计划，虽然第二次薪酬激励计划行权条件更加合理而且均行权成功，但是引发了更为严重的问题。由于万科股价被显著低估，甚至长期出现市场价格低于行权价格的情况，这导致股权激励缺乏吸引力。与此同时，由于股权激励需要员工自行出资购买来实现，行权成本巨大，进一步降低了行权的可能。而且创始人郁亮接任后，万科的业务重心由住宅转向商业地产所带来的内部震荡，大量高管离职。据统计，2011—2014年，万科共计4位执行副总裁、3位副总裁离职，累计离职的人数占激励对象的36%。加入其他地产公司、独立创业或转向热门的互联网公司，都是这些未能如期获得激励的高管的选择。

对于前两次薪酬激励计划的失败，郁亮进行了反思。他意识到，良好的薪酬激励计划应当激发管理层的主观能动性、工作热情和创造力，促使职业经理人共创、共享并共同承担经营管理风险。由此，郁亮耗费了一整年时间悉心制定了事业合伙人机制，于2014年5月启动了第三次薪酬激励计划，1320位中高层管理者及普通员工成为首批事业合伙人。万科的事业合伙人制度包括三个部分：一是合伙人持股计划，事业合伙人均签署委托协议，将其在经济利润、奖金及集体奖金账户中的全部收益委托给第三方基金管理机构盈安合伙基金，由其从二级市场购入万科A股票，并授权其引入融资杠杆进行投资，而盈安合伙基金在此时管理了大概4%的万科股票；二是事业跟投计划，对于新增项目，项目的直接管理者应跟随公司一起投资，其他员工可自愿参与跟投；三是事件合伙人管理，公司可以针对某一项事件，临时组成事件合伙人群组参与问题解决，该群组可以超越传统职责划分，通过跨部门协调来寻找最优方案，而待事件解决后，事件合伙人又回到各自的部门。这样，万科得以将项目管理层级扁平化，解决各部门之间各司其职、缺乏协调机制的问题。

事业合伙人制度的实施，显著激发了万科的中高层管理者的积极性。自2014年开始，万科的财务绩效持续好转，股价也稳健攀升。究其原因，权力下放和激励对象的身份转变是关键。在事业合伙人制度下，受激励对象获得了更大的自主权，成为企业某项业务的管理者和风险承担者。由于绑定了利益和风险，事业合伙人能够充分发挥能动性。

3. 沸沸扬扬的"宝万之争"

在事业合伙人制度初见成效，万科业务蒸蒸日上时，万科却遭遇到自成立以来最大的控制权危机——"宝万之争"。2015年，我国房地产市场出现积压，国家着手制订措施激励低迷的房地产行业。与此同时，我国股市低迷，万科股价大跌。这引起了宝能系掌门人姚振华的注意。宝能系得名于深圳的宝能集团，该集团以金融业、综合物业开发、现代物流产业等为核心。

2015年7月10日，宝能系通过旗下前海人寿购入5.53亿股万科股票，但并未引起万科注意。此后宝能系通过多种渠道高杠杆募集资金，持续购得26.81亿股万科股票，并以24.26%的持股轻松取代持股15.29%的华润，登上万科第一大股东宝座。宝能系在短短几个月内耗资数百亿元对万科的大规模增持，令万科管理层措手不及，也令市场震惊。对于宝能系的收购意向，王石明确表示反对。他认为万科是中国混合所有制企业的标杆，第一大股东理应是国有企业，而宝能系不具备成为万科大股东的资格。王石的观点反映了万科管理层的看法：鉴于宝能系收购南玻A后撤换管理层的激进做法，宝能系一旦入主万科，万科的管理层很可能会遭受大面积解雇。而对于广大投资者来说，若宝能系控股万科，必然会颠覆万科稳健专注的经营策略。

2015年12月18日，为遏制宝能系的增持势头，万科管理层以拟实施"重大资产重组"为由，申请万科A股停牌，并紧急召开会议商讨对策，尝试寻求"白衣骑士"入主万科，驱赶宝能系。然而，王石多次请求大股东华润增持万科股份，却遭到了华润的董事长傅育宁的拒绝，不得不另辟蹊径。2016年1月15日，万科发布了申请继续停牌的公告，声称在停牌期间，万科已与潜在交易方签署了合作意向书，申请继续停牌以完成进一步核查。2016年3月12日，万科发布公告，表明已与深圳市属大型国有独资企业深圳市地铁集团有限公司（以下简称深圳地铁）签署合作备忘录，双方拟以万科向深圳地铁新发行股份的方式，进行交易对价400亿～600亿元的重大资产重组。宝能系与华润先是对这一方案表示默许，但事后又突然表示反对。2016年6月23日，宝能系发表声明，明确表达对万科引入深圳地铁的反对意见，并表示将在8月股东大会上投出反对票。而华润也一反常态，通过其集团官方微信号声援宝能系，表示反对万科管理层提出的重组预案，仅支持万科与深圳地铁进行业务合作，并质疑万科董事会在审议及表决预案过程中的合规性及有效性。

在关键时刻，万科的独立董事华生表达了对华润与宝能系的反对，华生认为，首先，万科的成绩，与在华润长期默许下万科形成了完善的现代企业管理制度密不可分，而自宝能系举牌以来，华润不仅未与万科管理层沟通，反而开始一反常态地干预企业管理框架并破坏管理生态，极不可取。其次，华润以重组意向书中部分资产估价不合理为由反对重组，缺少格局，过于短视。再次，相对于能够给万科带来优质资产的深圳地铁，在各方面都远远落后于万科的宝能系地产不仅无法帮助万科发展，反而会带来同业竞争、利益冲突等一系列问题。最后，华润反对重组事项，却无法提出替代方案。若在华润干涉下万科与深圳地铁的重组失败，万科股价下跌，华润将无法保护中小投资者的利益不受损失。

2016年6月26日，宝能系向万科发出召开临时股东大会的申请，提议罢免现任万科董事长王石、总裁郁亮等10名董事和2名监事。而万科董事会则以拖延来消极应对。2016年7月4日，万科A股刚刚复盘，宝能系便再次购入万科股票并持股增至25%。根据万科章程，如果某一控制人能够增持至30%，将直接获得万科控股股东的身份。

正值此危急关头，万科最大的自然人股东向中国证监会等7部委发出公开举报信，对宝能系与华润进行了猛烈声讨，要求保护中小投资者权益。他主张宝能系与华润公开二者的利益关联和秘密协议，回应在深圳地铁重组方案上出尔反尔的理由，并呼吁二者做出不涉嫌内幕交易和市场操纵的声明，并指出宝能系涉嫌利用违法资金和不合规主体收购并控制上市公司。

2016年7月22日，证监会介入宝万之争。证监会约谈了万科及宝能系负责人，批评了双方的行为严重影响了公司的市场形象及正常的生产经营、违背了公司治理的义务，要求他们维护中小股东的利益、稳定资本市场秩序并恢复正常的企业运营。2016年12月5日，保监会发布信息，停止宝能系旗下前海人寿万能险的新业务。中国恒大于2016年8月4日起开始收购万科股份，直至持股14.07%。但中国恒大表示无意进一步控制万科股权，对万科的投资仅被账列为可供出售金融资产。2017年1月12日，华润发出公告，表明深圳地铁将全面收购华润及其子公司所持有的万科股票。2017年1月20日，该协议获得批准，深圳地铁获得了占万科总股本15.31%的股份,而华润获利退出;同年3月16日,中国恒大发布公告宣称将与深圳地铁进行战略合作,将其所占有的14.07%表决权委托给深圳地铁行使,期限一年。自此,在万科的股权结构中,作为万科现任管理团队及管理制度的支持者,深圳地铁(持股15.31%)、中国恒大(持股14.07%,且将表决权授予深圳地铁)、万科管理层及万科盈安合伙基金(共持股7.12%)及最大的自然人股东(持股1.21%)合计持股比例达到了37.71%。完全超过了届时持股约25.4%的宝能系,牢牢地稳固了公司的控制权。

2017年2月24日,保监会根据对宝能系旗下前海人寿的检查中发现的严重违法违规问题,对时任前海人寿董事长姚振华给予撤销任职资格并禁入保险业10年的处罚。

2017年6月30日,郁亮顺利当选万科新一届董事会主席,万科的管理团队及企业制度获得了稳定的延续。而伴随着宝能系对万科股权的逐渐转让,"宝万之争"彻底落下了帷幕。

4. 结语

纵观万科多年的发展,分散股权结构与职业经理人模式造就了万科独特的治理机制和先进的管理制度,也为其带来了一系列挑战与危机。经过了多次治理事件的洗礼,万科的股权结构更加集中,事业合伙人制度也取得了显著成效。而万科能否在房地产严格调控的新风向下稳健发展,则依然值得拭目以待。

案例问题:

1. 结合案例讨论,万科的分散股权结构对万科的治理有何影响?

【案例11】

2. 结合案例分析,不同类型的薪酬激励计划的优劣,讨论为何万科的合伙人计划可以取得成功。

3. 结合案例分析,董事会在公司治理之中的重要作用,并讨论独立董事的身份和角色。

4. 结合案例分析,万科在"宝万之争"的过程中主要使用了什么防御策略?

分析提示：

1. 分散股权及集中股权各有利弊。对于分散股权来说，其主要问题在于股东对于管理层缺乏控制，导致首要的委托代理问题位于股东与管理层之间，表现为董事会与管理层（尤其是 CEO）之间的冲突；而对于集中股权来说，其主要问题是大股东对于公司的高度掌控，导致首要的委托代理问题位于大股东与中小股东之间，表现为独立董事与内部董事和管理层成员之间的冲突。此外，股权高度集中的企业一般能够抵御外部市场的恶意收购；而股权分散的企业则可能面临较高的外部市场收购风险。

2. 薪酬激励计划是否有效涉及多方面的影响，如行权条件是否合理、行权的成本是否适宜、计划是否包含决策权分享，以及其他非经济激励措施等。因而，薪酬激励计划的有效性往往取决于计划和情境之间的匹配，完善的薪酬激励计划应当能对各种可能发生的情境予以考虑并提出相应的应对方案。

3. 董事会在不同情境下所发挥的作用是不同的。在企业运营正常时，董事会在常规的管理活动中并不发挥显著作用。但当公司发生严重的公司治理事件的过程中，董事会就成为公司控制权争夺的主战场。在这个过程中，董事席位的争夺直接决定了股东的利益及话语权。根据我国相关法律法规的规定，独立董事被定位为不依附于大股东的独立力量，在大股东之间、大股东与中小股东利益出现纷争时能够起到仲裁人的作用，从而对公司内部利益纷争的走向产生至关重要的影响。当然，在许多国内上市企业中，独立董事不一定会通过"提出异议""否决"等行为与大股东对抗，而更可能采用"弃权""缺席"或者"辞职"的方式来消极抗议大股东。

4. 防御策略的内涵广泛，常见的防御策略有"毒丸"（被恶意收购后，原股东有资格以折扣价购买新股或债券，从而稀释收购者的股权）、"金降落伞"（被收购后，收购者必须支付被收购公司的管理层成员巨额安置费）、"拖延"（利用董事会相关议程申请停牌、拖延召开股东大会）、"白衣骑士"（申请友好资本控股企业，驱逐恶意收购者）、"诉讼"（通过起诉收购者，分散其注意力和延缓其收购行为）。这些策略能够阻碍和迟滞恶意收购者的收购行为。

案例来源:

1. 杨翠兰. 冰冻三尺,非一日之寒:万科公司治理之重. 中国管理案例共享中心案例.

2. 范学俊,杜德,等. 收购万科,宝能资本大戏如何落幕?. 中国管理案例共享中心案例.

3. 胡杰武,陈翔,倪伟. 万科控制权之争之资产重组视角. 中国管理案例共享中心案例.

案例 12

小米公司的组织结构演化

知识点：

企业战略与结构的演化模式、业务层战略与职能结构的匹配、公司层战略与事业部制结构的匹配

案例目的：

本案例通过介绍小米公司自成立以来的战略与结构演变，引导学生理解企业战略与结构的协同演化，辨识不同特征职能结构与业务层战略的匹配，不同类型事业部结构与公司层战略的匹配，思考组织结构的设计原则。

案例正文：

2010年4月6日，在北京的保福寺桥银谷大厦，金山公司前任CEO、天使投资人雷军与六位联合创始人共同成立小米公司。

1. 势如破竹的新生企业

初创的小米实行全员持股，而创始人团队连同早期员工仅有56人。其中包括总裁雷军、副总裁林斌（原谷歌中国工程研究院副院长）、领导手机生产团队的周光平（原摩托罗拉中心高级总监）、领导手机工业设计团队的刘德（原北京科技大学工业设计系主任）、领导小米网及电商团队的黎万强（原金山词霸负责人）、领导MIUI系统开发团队的洪峰（原谷歌中国高级产品经理）和领导米聊团队的黄江吉（原微软中国工程院开发总监）。而手机、电商、MIUI系统及米聊软件，也正是小米初创阶段的四大核心业务。

为了降低市场风险，小米在成立之初并未直接进入手机行业，而是基于对安卓系统的深度优化，率先推出了操作系统MIUI和社交软件米聊，吸引了大量发烧级用户"米粉"通过MIUI社区、微博等方式参与MIUI系统的改善和打磨。对用户需求的细致了解，为小米设计制造第一款智能手机打下了基础。2011年10月，小米

正式发布双核 1.5GHz 智能手机小米 1，定价 1999 元，并限定仅在线上进行销售，首批 30 万台手机在 5 分钟内售罄。这种强大的需求让雷军看到了中国智能手机市场的广阔前景，也推动了小米的迅速发展。

2012 年，小米将手机的生产与工业设计融为一体，设立了手机部，小米网衍生出电商部，而 MIUI 系统和米聊软件也分别设立独立部门。为了保持小米的创造性，此时的小米采用了扁平化的组织结构，即顶层是小米的五位联合创始人，第二层是作为核心业务主管的中层部门经理，第三层是小米的基层员工。由于基层员工可以直接与用户互动，这有助于小米手机在研发过程中充分发掘并贴合用户需求。与此同时，小米针对不同的研发项目设立项目团队，而每位工程师都能申请成为项目主管。项目主管除了带领团队研发和进行日常管理，还需要负责与其他部门协调沟通。

借助扁平化的组织结构，小米的员工可以全身心地投入产品开发，充分发挥主观能动性，在灵活快速地响应客户需求的同时与公司的战略目标保持一致。因此，小米得以形成良性的工作氛围，创造出符合消费者需求的新颖产品。

2013 年 8 月 12 日，小米发布红米手机。当天，745 万用户参与预约，10 万台手机在 90 秒内被抢购一空。而在 2013 年"双十一"期间，小米单店破亿速度第一，手机品牌关注度第一，手机类单店销售量第一。凭借令人惊叹的业绩，小米在 2013 年实现了新一轮的融资，市场估值高达 100 亿美元。

2. 多元化与国际化的阵痛

2013 年，雷军着手推进硬件的多元化。在内部，小米开始布局流量入口级别的硬件，着力发展小米电视、小米盒子及路由器业务。为此，小米成立了小米盒子及电视部，减弱了对米聊软件的进一步开发，成立了路由器及云服务部。而在外部，小米通过风险投资的方式布局智能硬件领域，打造"生态链计划"。这一计划意在扩张小米产品线，尝试通过小米模式切入上百个细分领域，带动整个智能硬件产业的发展。此后，小米成立了生态链部，先后推出小米耳机、充电宝、手环、血压计、空气净化器和智能家具套装。截至 2016 年年底，小米共投资了 77 家智能硬件生态链公司，其中 30 家已发布产品，16 家年收入过 1 亿元，3 家年收入过 10 亿元，4 家估值超过 10 亿美元，总共积累了超过 7000 件产品专利。在开发生态链硬件的同时，小米还联合金山公司于 2014 年年底向世纪互联公司投资 2.3 亿美元，抢先布局云服务及大数据业务。由此，小米原先的"手机、电视、路由器"战略升级为"手机、电视、路由器 + 生态链"的新战略。

为了适应多元化的业务结构，小米采用事业部组织结构与网络型组织结构的混合模式。除法务、内部管理、公关及财务投资等职能部门外，电商部、路由器和云服务部、MIUI 部、小米盒子及电视部等业务部门均采用了事业部制，而小米生态链部和小米互娱部则采用了矩阵式的网络型结构——以小米公司为核心联结了一系列相对独立的生态链企业进行孵化。

与此同时，小米也开展了稳健的国际化之路。小米引进了谷歌安卓全球副总裁巴拉负责国际化拓展，通过与当地运营商签订合约机销售协议、借助网络宣传与线下销售结合等方式，小米快速进入新加坡、马来西亚、菲律宾、印度、巴西和印度尼西亚市场。而凭借在新兴国家市场的成功经验，小米手机随后攻入欧美市场，并借助低端机型进入非洲市场。

然而，正当小米的重心放在生态链及多元化时，小米的核心业务——手机却出现了严重的问题。由于小米手机最初以高性价比为卖点，相关技术储备较弱，这使得小米模式容易被模仿和参照。在小米模式获得成功后，魅族、一加、荣耀等国产品牌纷纷借鉴该模式推出一系列高性价比手机，并通过线上宣传结合线下渠道迅速占领了市场。而小米的芯片、屏幕等核心部件的供应未能跟上，影响了新机的发售和后续的出货。2015 年，小米出货的增速仅为 6.18%，市场占有率降至第四；2016 年，出货量出现下跌，市场占有率跌出前五。不仅如此，小米的信誉也受到负面新闻的影响，如印度专利禁令等。

面对逆境，从 2016 年 5 月开始，雷军主抓手机供应链，并重新调整了手机部门负责人的人选。此后，小米接连推出具有里程碑意义的高端全面屏手机小米 MIX、大屏手机小米 Note4，重塑了小米手机产品线。2016 年 7 月 7 日，在小米手机部全员动员大会上，雷军宣布吹响第二次创业的号角。此后，雷军力图为小米品牌赋予高性能与时尚性的身份，由红米品牌来承载高性价比。

在克服危机的过程中，小米重新梳理了组织架构。随着小米的业务范围与复杂度不断攀升、业务链条的延伸，小米出现了机构冗余复杂、管理幅度过大、协调管理困难的弊病。为此，小米开始简化机构，实施科层化改革。科层化改革细化了员工职能、促进了专业分工、降低了管理幅度，但是大部分研发技术类、企业内部管理类、产品类，以及决策部门依旧维持着扁平化结构。

3. 新起点与新出发

2018 年 7 月 9 日，小米成功上市，并开启了"泛硬件 + 新零售 + 互联网服务"的新铁三角战略。在泛硬件方面，新战略突出智能手机及核心硬件产品作为小米流量入口；在新零售方面，新战略强调借助小米之家的线下渠道与小米商城的线上渠道对生态链产品进行全面铺开；而在互联网服务方面，新战略则注重开发 MIUI 系统、广告业务、米家有品与金融服务以获取服务增值。与此同时，小米也确立了以云计算为核心，生态链为主轴的多元化方针。

为了贯彻小米新的战略部署，雷军再次对小米的组织结构进行改革。2018 年 7 月 31 日，小米对生态链部进行了组织结构调整。由于生态链部业务进一步丰富，人员进一步增加，此前扁平的管理协调十分困难。这次调整之后，生态链部进一步层级化，不仅增设了投资部、探索产品部和贵金属部等多个职能部门，原有的供应链、业务分析、品控及结构团队也被进一步细化为更为专业的职能部门。

2018 年 9 月 13 日，小米进行了上市之后最大的一次组织架构调整。此次调整的基本思路是分置决策、组织与职能部门，横向拓展业务部门。在业务部门方面，将 MIUI 部部分研发团队归入手机部，其他的业务部门被重新拆分组合为：大家电部，（新）生态链部，笔记本电脑部、智能硬件部、小米 IoT（物联网）平台部，有品电商部，以及互联网（分别负责不同类别的软件开发及内容业务）部。新的业务部门表明小米的业务重心发生了转移。在职能部门方面，维持金融部与产业园区部等不变，原市场部（除公关团队）与销售服务部电商团队及新媒体组被整合为（新）

销售与服务市场部,而原市场部公关团队则升级为公关部。此次结构调整中,最关键的是增设了组织部与参谋部,将原本分散在各个部门的决策权与人事权向上集中,从而保证战略在实施过程中统一有序。因此,小米在进行科层化改革的同时,维持了扁平化管理的原有优势。

2018年12月,为解决小米手机在国内销售长期没有起色的问题,雷军对销售与服务部进行了全面重组。他将原有的销售与服务市场部拆分为两个部门,国内销售团队被整合为中国区,而国外销售团队(除单独设立印度小米的印度市场)则被整合为国际部。新调整的中国区突出了对于中国市场的高度重视,尤其加强了对于国内线下市场的开发和对高端机型销售的改善。2019年6月,为进一步加强小米手机在国内的销售管理,雷军兼任中国区总裁,并推行了对中国区业务的科层制改革。

4. 新战略与深度蜕变

雷军对手机部和人工智能部门进行了深度的架构调整,以贯彻小米新铁三角战略中"手机+AIoT(人工智能物联网)"的泛硬件双引擎战略。

2019年2月18日,雷军宣布调整手机部的组织结构,以提升小米手机的研发和创新能力,增强部件供应链的稳定性。在这轮调整中,设计部与质量部维持不变,原手机成本部改设为参谋部,全面负责运营、业务经营,以及成本核算;原手机核心器件部改设为硬件研发部,增加了对音频器件的研发投入;同时增设了显示触控部,专门开发屏下指纹技术。同时,小米手机也调整为五大品牌:主攻中高端市场的小米、主攻青年及海外市场的红米、主攻印度市场的POCOPHONE,获得美图公司授权、主攻女性手机市场的美图手机,以及由小米投资、主攻专业游戏手机市场的黑鲨。

2019年2月26日,为了提升AIoT、AI和云技术的战略高度,小米增设了集团技术委员会,并随后进一步增设了AIoT战略委员会,用来协调整个小米公司各类产品开发中应用AI技术、IoT技术的方向和标准。与此同时,小米原来的人工智能与云平台团队增设为:负责AI技术与小爱产品的人工智能部,负责大数据、搜索及推荐业务的大数据部,以及负责云技术、小米云和运营维护的云平台部。与此同时,小米还进一步增设了负责海外应用开发的互联网五部，以及负责国内互联网商业化规划的互联网商业部。小米对 IoT 的发展进行了布局：在应用软件方面，开放的 IoT 云平台和米家 App 能够促进应用软件的开发和利用；在计算方面，可以借助金山云来实现发展；在通信网络方面，开发了小米盒子和小米路由器，能够有效连接各种终端；在交互设备方面，投资了超过 200 家小米生态链企业，2018 年接入网络的物联网设备高达 1.5 亿台。

随后，小米公司还改设了集团质量办公室，并于 2019 年 7 月增设了集团采购委员会和集团设计委员会。至此，小米重新梳理了职能结构，形成了职能层面的六个核心部门，即财务部、参谋部、组织部、质量委员会、采购委员会和技术委员会。此后，小米还对公司的组织框架进行了持续的调整，但基本的研发、销售及业务框架结构则趋于稳定。

5. 结语

2019 年，小米由 5 个项目团队及 56 名成员组成的创业企业，演化成为拥有 28 个职能及业务部门，容纳超过 17000 名全职雇员的庞大跨国企业集团。适宜的组织结构和卓有成效的战略相辅相成，促进了小米绩效的又一次迸发。数据显示，2021 年第二季度，小米全球市场业务持续突破，市场收入创历史新高，达到 436 亿元，同比增长 81.6%；小米智能手机出货量排名全球第二，市场占有率达 16.7%，其中，在 22 个国家和地区，小米智能手机的市场占有率排名第一。

【案例 12】

案例问题：

1. 结合案例分析，企业战略与结构协同演化的大致次序是什么？在小米公司的发展过程中如何体现？

2. 结合案例分析，扁平化结构与科层化结构各自有什么优点与缺点。为何小米创始时采取全面扁平化，而在成长后采取了扁平化与科层化并行的结构？为何小米不会全面推行科层化？

3. 结合案例分析，小米数次重组业务部门结构的逻辑是什么？为何在一些部门使用事业部制，而在另一些部门仍保持常规结构？

4.结合案例分析，小米调整业务结构的速度和幅度为何在2018年上市后显著加速。未来小米的结构调整会逐渐收敛还是会持续进行？

分析提示：

1.企业战略与结构协同演化的次序大概为，简单结构（聚焦战略）—职能结构（扁平化结构适用于差异化战略，层级化结构适用于成本领先战略，混合型结构则适用于整体成本领先/差异化战略）—事业部制结构（竞争型模式适用于非相关多元化，合作型模式适用于相关约束型多元化，而战略业务单元模式则适用于相关联系型多元化）。读者可依照这一次序对比小米的发展历史。

2.扁平化结构的优点是响应性好、对创新的包容性强，适用于研发及决策部门；科层化结构的优点是分工明确，专业性强，管理的统一性高，适用于任务容易拆分但规模庞大的业务部门。

3.业务重组一般是为了解决不同业务之间无法形成协同效应，管理协调成本过高的问题。为了进行业务重组，企业的组织结构也需要适应这一趋势。事业部制的优势是为部门提供独立发展与独立决策的空间和机会，并可以独立核算收益与利润，因而可以通过财务绩效对其表现进行衡量。而由于某些部门的工作难以独立核算其收益及利润，这些部门只能使用战略绩效的方式进行考核，而不能采用事业部制进行简单的财务评价。

4.企业的结构需要与环境和企业战略相适应。当企业所在环境复杂多变时，企业的结构也会有较为明显的频繁的变动。如果组织中相关业务所面临的不确定性较小、业务内容稳定，那么与以上业务相关部门的结构也将趋于稳定。

案例来源：

1.郭名媛，张岁婕，小米的进阶之路：专利管理实现战略转型.中国管理案例共享中心案例库教学案例.

2. 王荣森，解庆庆. 昨天已是历史，明天还很神秘：小米科技战略转型之路. 中国管理案例共享中心案例.

3. 马杰，王汝. 绘蓝图勇争锋：格力与小米之争. 中国管理案例共享中心案例.

案例 13

国企创业家任建新与中国化工

知识点：

战略领导力、战略领导者、关键战略领导行为、管理层继任

案例目的：

本案例通过介绍企业家任建新创建与发展中国化工的故事，引导学生分析领会战略领导力的本质，辨别关键战略领导行为，并思考管理者继任为企业带来的可能影响。

案例正文：

从西北升起的"蓝星"

1984年，在西北兰州的化工部化学机械研究院（以下简称化机院）担任团委书记的任建新发现了一组奇怪的数据：中国每年因锅炉结垢会多消耗850万吨原煤，而根本原因是我国工业清洁技术的落后。看到它，任建新突然想起"Lan-5"技术，理论上可以解决锅炉结垢的问题。"Lan-5"，全称"硝酸用工业缓蚀剂"，是化机院科研人员耗费5年时间研制出来的缓蚀剂，曾获得国家技术发明三等奖，却被长期搁置在档案室无人问津。此时，中国并没有本土工业清洗企业，所有涉及工业清洗的项目都被外国公司包揽。面对国内工业清洗市场的空白，任建新以家产做抵押向单位借款1万元，获准以"集体承包"的性质创办清洗公司，就这样，在研究院的防空洞里成立了中国蓝星（集团）股份有限公司（以下简称蓝星）。

由于"Lan-5"技术能够彻底清洗煤垢，大幅度提升锅炉的使用寿命，创业第一年，蓝星创造了32万元产值。

鉴于蓝星的价格低廉、效果优异，蓝星业务快速发展，"Lan-5"技术也推广至各行各业。1988年后，蓝星包揽了国家"七五"至"十五"期间从国外引进的石油、石化、化工、有色冶金、电力的大型成套装置开车前清洗业务。几年之间，蓝星迅

速扩张，成长为中国清洗技术门类最齐全、清洗综合应用能力最强的专业清洗公司。

在工业清洗业务供不应求、收益快速增长的情况下，任建新认为中国即将迎来大规模的工业化进程，迫切需要一个成熟的工业清洗行业，而单凭蓝星无法满足全国的需求。由此，任建新选择面向全国推广工业清洗技术。1994年，全国掌握清洗技术的企业达到上千家，清洗行业从业人员近3万人，为国家创造效益近百亿元。

磨砺中前进的中国蓝星

1996年，蓝星第一家上市公司——"蓝星清洗"在深交所成功上市。为了让企业获得更为宽广的发展空间，任建新申请将蓝星总部搬到北京。1996年年底，原化学工业部部长顾秀莲为蓝星公司揭牌。迁后的蓝星获得了更加广阔的发展空间与机遇。在工业清洗市场逐渐走向饱和后，蓝星决心通过兼并收购来寻找新的业务增长点。与此同时，国内存在着一些规模较大、运营困难的老旧国有化工企业，如果能够兼并收购并重整这些国有资源，蓝星的规模和业务将得以快速扩大。由此，以国企脱困为切入口，任建新主动担任化工部改革与管理小组组长，自1996年开始推动了蓝星对老旧国有化工企业的并购。

蓝星的第一个并购目标是以有机硅为主要产品的星火化工厂。虽然有机硅是发展尖端科技不可或缺的高技术材料，但此时我国却不能规模化生产。为打破国外对有机硅生产的垄断，星火化工厂引进了万吨级有机硅装置，5年试车28次，但次次都以失败告终，导致高达1.4亿元的巨大损失，负债率高达200%，超过一万名职工及家属员工没有收入，纷纷离岗谋生。

面对位于破产边缘的星火化工厂，任建新决定从企业管理和技术入手实施关键变革。为了了解企业的一手真实情况，任建新通过各种方式与一线工人直接接触。面对历史遗留问题，星火化工厂推行了历史上第一次全员下岗和重新竞聘，以实现减员增效。为实现生产线的成功运行，任建新从国外搜集并带回了大量技术资料，召回了大批离岗的技术骨干，还邀请了国内外多个专家来论证改造方案。经过5个月的刻苦攻关，第29次试车成功，中国也成为全球第五个能够规模化生产有机硅的国家。

通过兼并星火化工厂，蓝星成功开启了化工新材料的业务。此后经过四轮大规模兼并重组，蓝星陆续收购了南通合成材料厂、晨光化工研究院等多家国有化工企业和科研院所。在带领一众国有企业实现脱困奇迹的同时，蓝星成为化工新材料产业的龙头老大，企业资产直线突破200亿元，其中，双酚A与特种环氧树脂产值全国第一，有机硅产值全国第一、世界第三。

在并购大量化工企业后，为了整合优化业务结构，蓝星一度裁掉了超过四成员工。但是，任建新努力为下岗员工创造新的再就业机会，通过投资"马兰拉面""中车汽修"等业务，安置了大量下岗员工和职工家属。

走向世界的中国化工

2002年，蓝星升级成为国资委直接管理的国有大中型企业。面临着中国加入WTO后即将到来的激烈国际竞争，任建新向国家经贸委提出了建设中国"大化工"的建议，即进一步收购和整合在全国各地化工企业，建设类似中国石油、中国石化的大型企业集团，全面提升竞争力。2004年，蓝星与中国昊华化工集团股份有限公司重组为中国化工集团有限公司（以下简称中国化工），继续由任建新担任总经理。中国化工成立后，任建新提出了"老化工，新材料"的战略定位，其核心就是既不和上游争资源，也不和下游争市场，努力实现双赢或多赢，走一条行业和谐发展的价值创造之路。

为了进一步提升中国化工的技术竞争力，任建新启动了从本土企业向全球化公司的新一轮升级，而海外并购就成为主要手段。基于蓝星于20世纪90年代在国外成立合资公司所历练的国际化视野及蓝星在国内并购中所形成的并购能力，中国化工开始筹备海外并购。为保证海外并购的成功，中国化工聘请了世界一流的专业服务机构和专家，而且引进了美国最大的私募基金公司黑石集团作为战略投资者。在充分筹备后，任建新将并购目标设定为全球领先的化工细分领域龙头企业。自2006年开始，中国化工先后收购了法国、英国、德国等国家的行业领先企业，取得了显著的协同效应和良好的绩效。其中，2006年收购的世界三大营养添加剂企业法国安迪苏公司，截至2016年销售收入增长4倍，利润增长22倍，并实现了国内上市；

2011年收购的农药企业以色列安稻麦公司，截至2016年利润增长2倍以上，成为世界第六大农药企业。任建新认为，中国化工海外并购之所以成功，是因为文化融合，而实现文化融合的关键在于尊重和学习。截至2017年，任建新在完成了中华人民共和国成立以来最大的一笔海外并购，用430亿美元收购了在农业化工领域仅次于孟山都和杜邦的先正达。借此机会，中国化工成功跻身全球农业化工第一梯队，在种子与农药领域为中国的粮食安全打下了坚实的基础。

在这一系列海外收购完成后，中国化工"材料科学、生命科学、先进制造加基础化工"的"3+1"主业格局越发清晰。在经营管理这些海外世界级化工企业的过程中，中国化工不断汲取宝贵知识与经验，全面提升了技术水平和管理能力。

中国中化的新征程

2018年6月，任建新宣布退休，中国化工董事长的职位由中国中化集团有限公司（以下简称中化集团）董事长宁高宁兼任。虽同为并购专家，宁高宁的管理风格与任建新不同，相对于任建新保持海外并购企业高度独立运营的温和策略，宁高宁更注重在海外企业并购中实施大规模的深度整合。2021年5月，中国化工与中化集团宣布重组合并，成立了巨无霸企业"中国中化控股有限责任公司"（以下简称中国中化），宁高宁继续担任董事长。

作为全球规模最大化工品消费国与生产国，我国化工业相比发达国家还存在着精细化程度低、科技水平低、信息化与综合集成率低等问题，在高端化工产品方面严重依赖进口。而成立后的中国中化，作为一家真正的综合性大型跨国化工企业，将肩负着扭转这一局面，向巴斯夫股份公司、拜耳集团等国际化工巨头发起挑战的使命。

【案例13】

案例问题：

1.结合案例，领会什么是战略领导力？为何战略领导力对企业至关重要？

2.结合案例，识别任建新的领导行为体现了哪些关键战略领导行动？

3.结合案例思考,来自外部且管理风格与前任显著不同的企业领导者,将会给企业带来什么样的变化。

分析提示:

1.战略领导力是指预测事件、展望未来、保持灵活性并促使他人进行所需的战略变革的能力。

2.关键战略领导行动一般包含五个方面:确定战略方向、有效地管理公司的资源组合、维持一种有效的组织文化、强调道德准则和建立平衡的组织控制。

3.来自外部的管理层继任者一般会带来显著的战略变革。

案例来源:

饶恒.白手起家、低调退场,国企创业家任建新.中国质量,2019,(04):93–97.

案例 14

羽绒国货波司登的战略性创业之路

知识点：

创业机会、公司内部创业、战略性创业、发明、创新、模仿

案例目的：

本案例通过对波司登内部创业过程的分析，引导学生理解创业机会，思考战略性创业的过程。

案例正文：

2019年11月27日，中国羽绒服品牌领导者波司登和法国品牌高缇耶合作推出联名系列，吸引了时尚明星与行业大咖的广泛关注，更是成为时尚媒体的热议焦点。

波司登最早创立于1976年。1992年，创始人高德康大胆引进先进生产流水线，创立"波司登"品牌。从1995年起，波司登连续15年销售额保持中国羽绒服行业第一。2007年，波司登成为中国羽绒服装行业第一家在港交所上市企业，实现了从"中国名牌"向"世界名牌"的飞跃。然而，自2010年起，波司登却陷入了企业发展以来最大的困境。

1. 深陷危机的波司登

第一，波司登遭遇来自国内和国际的多重竞争压力。在国内方面，森马、雅戈尔、七匹狼等大举进入羽绒服市场，凭借款式、版型、色彩设计和主流渠道上的优势，逐步蚕食羽绒服市场。同时，李宁、安踏等也推出运动羽绒服系列。在国际方面，优衣库等也在羽绒服业务展开新的布局，甚至阿玛尼等也加速在亚太地区羽绒市场的扩张。

第二，波司登面临市场需求的巨大变化，原有品牌快速老化。随着波司登的羽绒服存在着样式单一、销售模式落后、新产品开发不足等问题，导致整体品牌形象

弱化，逐渐沦为消费者心中"妈妈辈穿的羽绒服"。此外，波司登的经营管理也积累了诸多问题。例如，线下门店存量巨大且迅速扩张，使公司无法及时获取最新市场信息，再加上产品种类布局不够合理，不能满足消费者需求。多种因素的叠加使得波司登深受产能过剩、库存的拖累，资金链高度脆弱。2013—2016年，整个服装行业陷入寒冬期，波司登营业收入从接近百亿元，一路跌至60亿元以下。2014年，在宏观经济增速放缓，服装行业整体下滑以及市场竞争加剧的大背景下，波司登在渠道方面的一系列努力并没有缓解库存压力，2016年，波司登净利润仅为1.38亿元。与此同时，公司股价也从之前的每股4港元左右，一路下跌至在0.4港元附近徘徊。因此，波司登不得不改变企业战略。

2. 波司登的"二次创业"

2018年，波司登引入外部战略咨询力量，系统梳理和反思自身特点和传统战略，决定全面启动战略转型。在品牌方面，相较于同行企业，波司登的优势在于领先同行的技术积累和良好的口碑。在顾客认知方面，波司登已成为羽绒服品类的代名词，这是波司登的核心优势。在研发方面，自1976年以来，波司登凭借出色的产品生产制作工艺，引领了行业三次羽绒服革命，累计持有177项专利，参与了5项国际标准、9项国家标准和4项行业标准的制定。可见，雄厚的研发实力能够为波司登产品的品质提供重要支撑。

围绕核心战略"聚焦主航道，聚焦主品牌"，下定决心转变的波司登采取了一系列措施，包括激活品牌、升级产品、优化渠道等。

波司登开始重新梳理、建立品牌公关活动与产品，调整营销推广的节奏，对年度新开发产品及核心主打产品进行资源投入。羽绒服是功能性产品，在主体功能保暖的同时，时尚、潮流是未来的趋势。因此，波司登一鼓作气推出了多个系列，如米兰时装周系列、IP联名系列等。2018年7月18日，波司登斥巨资在北京水立方举行发布会，成为服装行业唯一入选国家品牌计划的企业。

波司登积极推进品牌国际化，将卓越的设计与典雅的中国元素带向国际时尚舞台。波司登凭借优质的设计、前瞻性的艺术审美与先锋的时尚触觉，向世界展示中国服装品牌的魅力、强大自信和时尚态度。例如，波司登作为独立品牌受邀参加2018年纽约时装周，举行新品发布秀，目的在于改变消费者对品牌的固有认知。这次国际秀引发了全球同行业、媒体与消费者对波司登的热议，获得了媒体与消费者的正面评价。

围绕着品牌定位，波司登也在产品、销售渠道和运营等方面进行了变革。在产品研发方面，波司登根据市场流行趋势、消费需求，以及公司品牌战略，加强公司各部门之间的沟通，确保产品研发方向与公司品牌战略一致。在产品创新方面，波司登成立了品质升级委员会，对研发、技术、销售和售后服务多个环节进行管控。其中，波司登尤其重视产品的研发升级，在现有的基础上，全面提升面料、绒、毛、辅料品质和生产工艺，如波司登推出的"极寒"高端功能系列。

波司登积极优化零售网络，关闭低效店铺，提升单店质量。2017年，波司登羽绒服零售网点由221家增加至4513家，自营零售网点由58家增加至1432家，第三方经销商经营的零售网点由163家增加至3081家。同时，波司登还持续加大对终端店铺和加盟商的支持力度，改造升级终端店铺，提升消费者购物体验。针对之前一直被忽略的门店设计模块，波司登专门聘请法国顶尖设计团队重新设计门店，提升消费者对波司登的感官体验。线下门店是消费者认知品牌、感受产品、完成消费闭环的重要场所。目前，波司登已入驻杭州大厦、凯德、万象城、新天地等主流商业体。

波司登大胆探索数字化运营，提前布局未来新场景。2020年以来新冠肺炎疫情之下，线下门店营业受到冲击，物流配送也存在诸多限制，各行各业的营收都受到了极大的影响。面对此种情况，波司登迅速调整自身状态，积极推进数字化转型，聚焦新零售能力建设、商品快反能力建设和数据中台建设，将数字化应用到用户、品牌、产品、渠道、零售、人资、财务等经营过程中。通过数字化，波司登打通了产销互动的渠道，精准描绘消费者画像，并对其进行精准营销，有效发挥数字化赋能品牌价值增长的作用。

3. 波司登的再度崛起

以"全球热销的羽绒服专家"为竞争战略新方向,波司登激活了品牌的内在生长力,也拉动了产品、渠道等全面升级,成功扭转了市场的不利局面,实现稳健增长。据调查,2017年以前,波司登30岁以下顾客群体占比不足11%,2019年,该数据已提升至近30%,品牌年轻化、时尚化的转型取得了明显进展。2020年,波司登营业收入突破121.9亿元,再创历史新高,同比增长17.4%,羽绒服规模总量跃居全球第一;毛利由上年同期的55.1亿元增加21.7%至67.1亿元。

【案例14】

案例问题:

1. 波司登如何发现并把握创业机会?
2. 波司登如何发展公司内部创业?
3. 战略性创业如何帮助波司登创造价值?

分析提示:

1. 创业机会是指新产品和新服务能够满足市场需求的情形。创业机会可能以不同方式出现,如开发和销售新产品的机会,或者在新市场上销售现有产品的机会。在本案例中,波司登具有创业意识,善于发现并把握创业机会,取得了巨大的商业成功。此问题可以从识别已有创业机会和开发新的创业机会两个角度进行分析。

2. 公司内部创业是指在位企业发现新机会、利用新机会并创造新价值的过程。在本案例中,波司登为了摆脱日趋激烈的同质化竞争困境,开展了一系列自上而下和自下而上的内部创业行动。此问题可以从自发性战略行为和引导性战略行为的角度进行分析。

3. 战略性创业既可以是渐进式创新,也可以是突破式创新。在本案例中,波司登的渐进性创新更多,突破性创新偏少。但是,突破性创新能够创造更多销售收入和利润,特别是为顾客、股东等利益相关者创造更大价值。此问题可以根据战略性创业的类型,对战略性创业促进波司登创造价值的情况进行分析。

案例来源：

黄海昕，高翰，马晓蕾.温暖全世界：梦想如何照亮波司登战略创业之路.中国管理案例共享中心案例.

Case 1

A Brief Analysis of Longzhong Dialogue's Strategic Management Thoughts

Key points:

Strategic management process;Adaptability of environment and strategy

Case Purpose:

Students are guided to understand the strategic management process and think about the adaptability of the environment and strategy through the analysis of the strategic management thoughts contained in *Longzhong Dialogue*.

Case Description:

Since the dictatorship of Dong Zhuo, numerous powers have arisen and conquered various regions and provinces across the country. Among them, Cao Cao is far less renowned and has far fewer militaries compared with Yuan Shao. But Cao Cao wiped out Yuan Shao, defeating the many and strong with the few and weak, because of not only favorable timing, but also his competent think tank. Now Cao Cao has an aggregate of some one million forces and is holding the emperor as a puppet to command all the other powers in the country. As such, it is unwise to fight with him directly for the time being. Another powerful general, Sun Quan, has dominated Jiangdong Region as the third generation. Jiangdong has sophisticated terrains and people there are supporting Sun Quan. Moreover, he is a wise lord who knows to employ eligible people. Therefore, he should be regarded as backup instead of attack object. Jingzhou is adjacent to upstream of Han River in the north, Nanhai in the south, Wu and Kuaiji in the east, and Ba and Shu in the west. It has long been a strategic territory that are conquered by military opponents. However, Liu Biao, its owner, is not able to keep it. So, isn't it a gift of God for you? How do you think for it? In addition, Yizhou is surrounded by mountains of difficult access and has vast and fertile basin. The distinguished founder emperor of Han Dynasty relied on Yizhou to establish his imperial cause. Yet its owner Liu Zhang is fatuous and also threatened by Zhang Lu in the north. Though both the regime and its people are prosperous and wealthy, Liu Zhang never cherish them while the able and virtuous men all starve for the wise leader. Dear general, you are the descendant of the royal family, enjoy a renowned reputation around the country, and desire greatly to welcome heroes and gifted masterminds hospitably, so if you can occupy Jingzhou and Yizhou, safeguard the vital passes, forge a sound relationship with the minorities in the west, appease the minorities in the south, form an external union with Sun Quan and conduct internal political reform, once the situation changes, you can dispatch a senior general to lead the armies in Jingzhou to Nanyang and Luoyang while you in person lead the Yizhou armies to Qinchuan. I believe all the people in Qinchuan would happily embrace you with food and wine! If so, realization of the great cause and renaissance of Han Dynasty can be expected.

—Excerpt from *Zhuge Liang Biography, Records of the Shu Kingdom, Records of the Three Kingdoms*

More than 1800 years ago, Liu Bei visited Zhuge Liang's cottage thrice in succession. Zhuge Liang didn't accept Liu Bei's invitation until the third time and proposed to Liu Bei a strategic plan called in later times *Longzhong Dialogue*.

At the outset, Zhuge Liang made analysis to Liu Bei the entire market competition environment at that time. All major companies were competing for market share, and the competition was extremely fierce, this is the analysis of the external environment in strategic management.

Then Zhuge Liang analyzed Cao Cao as a competitor. Cao Cao was the adopted son of a eunuch, although his family was rich and distinguished, his reputation was not too great. Compared with Yuan Shao, his strength was very weak, his resources were poor, and his team was not strong, but he can grow from a weak person to a strong one. Not simply because he seized the opportunity, but because he had strategic thinking. Now Cao Cao has

Case 1　A Brief Analysis of Longzhong Dialogue's Strategic Management Thoughts

grown into a big power in the market. Therefore, he advised Liu Bei not to fight with him directly for the time being.

Zhuge Liang then analyzed Sun Quan, who was also a strong competitor for market share at that time. Sun Quan was rooted in Jiangdong for a long time, had a good market foundation, good customer loyalty, excellent soldiers, rich grains, and steep terrain which was conducive to combat. Besides, the Yangtze River was a natural barrier. Although he was a competitor, we can first form a strategic alliance and work together to fight against Cao Cao.

After analyzing the market competition situation, Zhuge Liang planned out Liu Bei's market space. Jingzhou, with a superior geographical location, was a province with connections in all directions. However, Liu Biao, who currently occupied this market, had no ambitions, short-sightedness, and low customer loyalty. When Zhuge Liang analyzed the strategic situation for Liu Bei, he put forward the threat in the external environment. Competitors were strong and external competition was fierce, but there were also breakthrough opportunities. This opportunity was Jingzhou which had not been firmly controlled by others, which was a good cake. Then, he gave another breakthrough opportunity—Yizhou. Yizhou was a fertile and big market. Some enterprises once occupied it and achieved a great cause in the history. But now Yizhou was controlled by Liu Zhang who had good customers but failed to provide them with corresponding services and meet their needs. Many talented people were ready to change jobs and hoped to display their capability in excellent enterprises. Isn't this a good opportunity for the general? In the previous half of the analysis, Zhuge Liang first analyzed the overall macro environment. The market competition was very fierce. Then, after analyzing the strength of competitors including Cao Cao and Sun Quan, he gave two strategic breakthroughs. One was Jingzhou, the other one was Yizhou.

After analyzing the external environment to Liu Bei, Zhuge Liang turned to analyze the internal environment. Liu Bei had the following internal resources and capabilities: "You are the descendant of the royal family" is equivalent to having a time-honored brand in the enterprise; "enjoy a renowned reputation around the country" represents that the team led by Liu Bei has a good reputation; "desire greatly to welcome heroes and gifted masterminds hospitably" displays good human resources in General Liu Bei's troop.

After analyzing the external and internal environment, Zhuge Liang pointed out a strategic path to Liu Bei: do a good job in internal management, go outside to ally with Sun Quan, and have a good relationship with some surrounding powers. In this way, he can occupy Jingzhou and Yizhou with which it would form a clamping effect on Cao Cao, and eventually unify the country. "If so, realization of the great cause and renaissance of Han Dynasty can be expected." This is Liu Bei's proposed vision and mission.

Longzhong Dialogue is a very classical strategic planning report in which Zhuge Liang pointed out the vision, mission and strategic goal of the company, "realization of the great cause and renaissance of Han Dynasty". How to formulate strategy specific for the goal? First, he analyzed the external environment, market environment and competitive environment, then analyzed the internal environment of resources and capabilities, identified opportunities, threats, advantages, and disadvantages, and finally formulated a strategy: seize Jingzhou and Yizhou, and take them as a base to form an alliance with Sun Quan to fight against Cao Cao, so as to achieve the strategic goal.

It was under the guidance of *Longzhong Dialogue*'s strategic planning that Liu Bei, who was suffering from domestic and foreign aggression and was down and out at that time, realized great cause of one Kingdom among the Three Kingdoms. However, no matter how perfect strategic planning is, it must be reviewed and changed over time. Due to the collapse of the Sun Quan and Liu Bei alliance as well as the scattered forces of Liu Bei, the *Longzhong Dialogue*'s strategic goal was only half achieved.

【Case 1】

Questions:

1. What are the content of the strategic management process in *Longzhong Dialogue*?

Case 1 A Brief Analysis of Longzhong Dialogue's Strategic Management Thoughts

2. What was Zhuge Liang's consideration in proposing to Liu Bei the strategic path of alliance with Sun Quan and seizing Jingzhou and Yizhou?

3. The strategic goal of "realization of the great cause and renaissance of Han Dynasty" had not been fully realized. What do you think the reason is?

4. Do you agree with the strategic thinking put forward by Zhuge Liang in "Longzhong Dialogue"? How to evaluate it?

Tips for answering the questions:

1. The strategic management process includes: vision, mission, strategic goals, internal and external environment analysis, strategy formulation, strategy implementation and adjustment. It is a closed-loop process.

2. The strategic path is proposed on the basis of environmental analysis and strategy formulation. Environmental analysis includes external environmental analysis and internal environmental analysis. Enterprises need to identify the opportunities and threats in the external environment, and the advantages and disadvantages in the internal environment, find the direction of strategy formulation and determine the strategic path through the strategic breakthrough.

3. Students can further analyze Liu Bei's internal and external environment at that time and consider the dynamics of the environment. When the environment changes, the strategy also needs to be adjusted accordingly. The achievement of strategic objectives is closely related to the environment in which the enterprise is located and the changes in the environment.

4. Strategic managers need to predict, adapt to, and even create changes in the changing environment, and win the enterprise competition in the change. The strategic decision

of the strategic manager is related to the situation at that time, as well as the strategic manager's grasp and judgment of the environment. Students may, based on the current situation, form their own judgments on strategic issues.

Case 2

Spring Airlines: the Great Cause of Low-cost Airlines

Key points:

Industry environment;Competitive advantage;Strategy;Strategy implementation;Strategic leader; Mission, vision; Organizational culture; Strategic management process

Case Purpose:

Through the analysis of the environment and strategy of Spring Airlines, the case guides students to understand the mission, vision and strategy implementation, and think about the important role played by strategic leaders.

Case Description:

The COVID-19 outbreak at the beginning of 2020 has plunged the global aviation industry into a vortex, and the consequent sluggish travel demand, insufficient capacity, and cash flow shortage have made the aviation industry reshuffling. However, in 2021, low-cost airlines have been the first to bottom out and rebound, returning to the level before the epidemic and achieving new growth. Among them, the outstanding performance of Spring Airlines as the pioneer of China's low-cost airlines is once again impressive.

In people's traditional concept, air travel has been a luxury choice for a long time, even a "privilege" exclusive to high-end consumer groups such as business people. From a market perspective, China's aviation industry has always been dominated by several large state-owned airlines such as China Southern Airlines, Eastern Airlines, and Air China. They are almost all high-priced full-service airlines.

In order to break the above situation, Spring Airlines successively introduced ultra-low-ticket fares in 2006 such as CNY 1, CNY 99, CNY 199, and CNY 299. In 2013, the Civil Aviation Administration of China and the International Civil Aviation Organization held a summit on the development and future of China's low-cost airlines, marking that the Chinese aviation industry has shifted from a luxury vehicle to a vehicle affordable to everyone. Air travel is neither a symbol of prestigious status, nor a display of luxury.

Low-cost airlines refer to some airlines that, on the premise of meeting flight safety standards, strip off some traditional airlines' services included in the fare, and provide paid services other than aviation displacement, thereby reducing the company's operating costs, reducing regular fares, attracting more passengers, and achieving the purpose of continuous operation. Low-cost airlines are based on low fares and insist on small profits but quick turnover, which has fundamentally changed the structure of the traditional aviation market. Today, low-cost airlines have swept major global aviation markets, and have become one of the fastest-growing sectors in the aviation industry.

In fact, as early as the 1970s and 1980s, 70%-80% of the short and medium flight in Europe belonged to low-cost airlines. In recent years, the development trend of low-cost aviation has been accelerated: on the one hand, traditional European companies such as the three major European airlines (British Airways, Lufthansa, and Air France) have specifically divested their low-cost aviation divisions to take over the short- and medium-haul businesses in Europe independently. On the other hand, low-cost airlines are booming all over the world, and a number of outstanding low-cost airline companies have emerged. For example, Southwest Airlines in North America, GOL Airlines in South America, Ryanair and Jetstar Airlines in Europe, AirAsia in Southeast Asia, Spring Airlines in China and so on.

From a worldwide comparison, although China's low-cost airline market started late and its existing market share is small, its potential demand is extremely large and it is ushering in explosive growth. At present, local or private small and medium-sized airlines in China have followed suit. domestic low-cost airlines mainly include: Spring Airlines, 9Air, Chengdu Airlines, West Air, Happy Airlines, Urumqi Airlines and Lucky Air.

Since Spring Airlines was officially put into commercial operation in July 2005, it has adhered to the low-cost strategy and pursued the concept of "everyone can fly", and has maintained profitability since its inauguration. By the end of September 2023, Spring Airlines had 122 Airbus A320 aircrafts with an average age of 7.0 years, covering major business and tourism cities in China, Southeast Asia, and Northeast Asia. It operates over 210 routes and transports 20 million passengers annually. The reason why Spring Airlines has achieved such impressive performance is mainly due to the clear corporate competitive strategy. When most domestic airlines lacked a clear and accurate market positioning, and were still "grabbing" high-end and low-end passengers in general, Spring Airlines had already clarified the positioning of low-cost air transportation market to serve the general public.

In order to effectively implement the low-cost strategy, Spring Airlines adheres to the "2S, 2H and 2L" business strategy, and on this basis, by occupying the domestic feeder market and using independent marketing channels to provide differentiated services to passengers, and then achieve expansion and profitability. "2S" refers to single aircraft type and single cabin system. The aircraft introduced by Spring Airlines are unified as Airbus A320. Through modification, the settings of first course and business course are cancelled, and only the economy course is available. In contrast, domestic airliners generally maintain the "two-cabin system" for business and economy. The single-type and single-cabin fleet reduces the cost of personnel license training, aviation material storage, and flight maintenance. "2H" refers to high passenger load factor and high aircraft utilization. Through the modification, the number of seats of Spring Airlines aircraft has increased to 186, which is 26 seats more than the average domestic passenger aircraft. This allows Spring Airlines aircraft to accommodate more passengers, and the cost per passenger is reduced by about 14%-15%. In order to achieve high utilization, Spring Airlines adopts a "point-to-point" route structure and arranges flights in a high-density manner in terms of route planning. Currently, Xiamen, Shenyang, Harbin, Qingdao, Guangzhou, Haikou, Sanya and other routes operate 2-4 flights every day. "2L" refers to low marketing costs and low management costs, including simplifying ground and cabin services, reducing free baggage weight, relying on Spring and Autumn International Travel's numerous outlets to book tickets, using telephone call centers or online direct sales, etc. These marketing methods reduce labor costs and operating expenses as much as possible.

Spring Airlines Chairman Wang Zhenghua has a catch phrase: "Profit comes half from earning half from saving." Wang Zhenghua's "frugal management" model has become an industry benchmark in terms of cost saving of Spring Airlines. Under this management model, Spring Airlines' main business costs are 62% lower than the industry average, management costs are 50% lower than the industry average, financial costs are 60% lower than the industry average, and marketing costs are 78% lower than the industry average. Regarding Spring Airlines' corporate strategy, Wang Zhenghua said frankly: "The first is to understand your advantages for appropriate positioning, the second is to stick to the goal after you determined."

Wang Zhenghua once led a team and visited low-cost airlines in the United Kingdom and the United States, fully learning their experiences and the potential of auxiliary business related to the core passenger transport business. At present, Spring Airlines' ancillary business mainly focuses on the sales of aircraft supplies, excess baggage charges, fast boarding and insurance commissions. In 2022, its auxiliary business revenue reached CNY 490 million.

Combined with the context of China's aviation industry, Spring Airlines has explored new experiences. Spring Airlines invested nearly CNY 20 million to develop its own ticketing system, encouraging passengers to buy tickets on its official website. Although this has also led to a relatively single ticket purchase channel for Spring Airlines, its official website often organizes ticket promotions. In order to facilitate passengers to purchase tickets, Spring Airlines also cooperates with Alipay, WeChat Pay and major banks. Besides, Spring Airlines has also developed its own departure system which consists of a passenger check-in system and a flight control system and allows passenger seat selection and registration.

Passengers can purchase tickets and choose seats at home without having to go through baggage check-in procedures. Spring Airlines also launched the "CNY 99 series of special air tickets" to attract target customer groups and improve customer loyalty and satisfaction. In 2013, Spring Airlines' independent electronic system saved more than CNY 280 million expenses for the company while when most domestic small and medium airlines still rely on traditional ticket agent system. The application of Spring Airlines' distribution system minimized the agency fees and other related expenses in the ticket sales process, and enhanced the independence of sales and control over the sales channels. It maintained a high percentage of ticket direct sales. At the same time, by maximizing the use of third-party service providers' resources and services in various airports, Spring Airlines reduced daily administration costs as much as possible. For example, Spring Airlines has only 5 management levels, which simplifies personnel relations to the greatest extent. It saved a lot of labor costs and maintained the cohesion of the entire enterprise. Through strict budget management, scientific performance appraisal and reasonable control of human-machine ratio, Spring Airlines has also effectively reduced the manpower cost and daily expenses of management personnel.

Questions:

1. In the aviation industry, how important is the environment's impact on airline performance? According to the industrial organization model (I/O model), give an analysis of how Spring Airlines obtains excess profits and share your understanding.

2. What are the important influences of founder Wang Zhenghua on Spring Airlines' strategy? How can strategic leaders succeed in the aviation industry?

Tips for Answering the Questions:

1. The I/O model of excess profit can explain the decisive influence of external environment on the company's strategic action. The I/O model emphasizes that compared

with the decisions made by managers within the organization, the industry segments that the company chooses to enter have a greater impact on its performance. In this case, in the face of the huge demand for domestic air travel, Spring Airlines chose the low-cost aviation strategy and obtained excess profits. Students can analyze the company strategy of Spring Airlines and the excess profits it has obtained on the basis of investigating the external environment, industry structure characteristics and its own resource advantages.

2. Strategic leaders refer to those who come from different departments and levels of the company, use the strategic management process to select strategic actions, and help the company realize its vision and fulfill its mission. The strategic leader has an all-round influence on the company. He not only dominates the general direction of the company's strategy, but also his personal decisions and actions will affect the shaping of the organizational culture. In this case, Wang Zhenghua, the founder of Spring Airlines, is a strategic leader. Students can focus on Wang Zhenghua's words and deeds to analyze his behaviors such as grasping the external environment, making decisions on the company strategy, and shaping the corporate culture.

Case 3

Fenghua Property: Strategic Transformation Following the Trend

Key points:

Macro environment; Industrial environment; Competitive environment

Case Purpose:

Based on a letter addressed by the Chairman of Fenghua Property Management Co., Ltd. to its shareholders, this case intends to guide the students to analyze the external environment, e.g. macro environment, industrial environment and competitive environment, and think about the adaptation of strategy to environment.

Case Description:

A Letter to Shareholders by Chairman of Fenghua Property Management Co., Ltd.

The Chairman of Fenghua Property Management Co., Ltd. addressed a letter to its shareholders at the 30th anniversary of its founding. The letter was extracted as follows:

As the first property management company locally, we, Fenghua Property Management Co., Ltd., were established in May 1991. With 30 years' development, we have grown into a highly reputable local brand recognized as one of the Top 100 property management enterprises in China, with over 18,000 employees and nearly 100 million square meters of property management area. Our employees are more united and loyal. Now under the nationwide expansion strategy, our footprint has extended from local areas to nationwide. The scope of property management businesses was more diversified, covering office buildings, buildings of government authorities, high-rise residential buildings, luxury villas, shopping malls, urban complexes, industrial areas, and scenic spots. We have achieved an unprecedented development speed and scale.

Such achievements were made mainly because Fenghua has always maintained high sensitivity and adaptability to the external environment and carried out change and transform in a timely manner. At the inception of founding, we were mainly engaged in the property management of old residential buildings. Later through transformation, we extended to mid-to-high-end residential properties. As the real estate market grew in rise, we won some local residential buildings projects and gradually gained a firm foothold in the market. However, continuous prosperity of local real estate market attracted a large number of property developers of other regions. Their property management branches seized considerable share in residential property management market and brought great pressure to local companies. At that time, the government proposed the concept of "Building Economy". Following such trend, we extended to office building property management business, which was our first transformation, from "residential property management" to "office building property management". The office building property management business created considerable revenue for us and became the most popular business of us. However, due to the influx of new competitors, oversupply of office buildings and the difficulty in collecting property management fees, we had to transform again, that is "service outsourcing" advocated by the government. We seized the opportunity in time and undertook a large number of governmental services projects. That is our second transition, from "office building property management" to "urban services." At present, the revenue from residential property management business only accounts for 10% of the total operating income of us, while that from urban services business mainly in government buildings and public properties has increased year by year to become the main revenue of us.

On this basis, we proposed our positioning as an "urban service provider" at the beginning of this year. In this transformation, we face more opportunities and greater challenges. From the perspective of opportunities, on the one hand, the scope of service outsourcing businesses of the government will gradually expand and offer greater room of operation and profitability, and on the other hand, the competition of urban services market in China is not yet fierce, and there is still a lot of businesses to compete for. From the perspective of challenges, the real estate market has shifted to stock market from incremental market and a large number of property management companies have turned their focus to public services or urban services business. Relying on their powerful financial and technical strength, they began to transform from traditional property management enterprises to modern property service providers to explore value-added services in property management. Under the support of real estate developers, these property management enterprises are highly tolerant to risks and very competitive in marketing. They are staring at the emerging market. For example, Country Garden Services has reached strategic cooperation with many cities including Zunyi, Hengshui and Xichang to promote the implementation of projects. On the other hand, some internet based, hi-tech and specialized companies are also very competitive in delivery of professional services, development of value-added services, and project management because of their clear positioning and market target.

At present, our business is growing rapidly because we chose the right direction of market transformation-to be an urban services provider. But how long will such a favorable situation last? Rapid expansion of the market has concealed many problems in development, for example although the company's revenue has increased year by year, the profit margin did not see a significant increase. We must consider and face these issues in the company's development towards an urban services provider.

Unlike traditional property management, urban services will incorporate more service patterns, including all services related to not only the traditional property management of communities and office buildings, but also urban operation, such as schools, hospitals, road cleaning, scenic spots, and highways. In other words, all services needed for urban operation will become the company's business. With the extension of scope of business, the competition situation will also undergo tremendous changes. What is an urban services provider? It is still a question worthy of everyone's consideration.

Questions:

【Case 3】

1. What strategic transformations has Fenghua carried out in its development of over 30 years?

2. What opportunities and challenges in the external environment did Fenghua encounter in its transformation towards an urban services provider?

3. Based on the case, describe why it is so important for the companies to study and understand the external environment.

Tips for answering the questions:

1. Every strategic transformation of Fenghua was accompanied by changes in the external environment. In combination with case, students can sort out several changes in the external environment, as well as the corresponding strategic transformation of enterprises, and think about the relationship between strategy and environment. Fenghua's strategic transformation may be considered from the perspective of transformation and upgrading of business items and scope.

2. As for the opportunities and challenges Fenghua encountered in the process of transformation to urban service providers, make analysis from the perspectives of macro environment, industrial environment and competitive environment in the external environment. Urban service providers refer to property management enterprises undertaking projects entrusted by the government to carry out property service activities for the purpose of serving urban management and operation. Students need to think about the influence of external environmental factors behind the gradual expansion of urban service business by some property management enterprises.

3. Review the case analysis process and the Five Forces Model and the Dynamic Competition Model used to further understand the dynamics of environment and the adaptability of strategy to environment.

Case 4

Yinfa: A Company in A Dilemma of Transformation and Upgrading

Key points:

Internal environment analysis; Core competence; Core resources; VRIO model

Case Purpose:

This case study is intended to analyze Ningbo Yinfa Green Food Co., Ltd. which is in a dilemma of selecting its development strategy. Through the development process of Yinfa, it is intended to guide the students to think about the internal resources and capabilities of a company, identify its advantages and disadvantages, and understand the adaptability of internal environment to the strategy.

Case Description:

1. Introduction

On December 11, 2018, Wang Yan (a pseudonym), the daughter and Zhao Jin (a pseudonym), the son-in-law of Wang Yong, founder of Ningbo Yinfa Green Food Co., Ltd. (hereinafter referred to as Yinfa) jointly knocked a gong at Ningbo Equity Exchange (NBEE). After the listing in NBEE, the financing ability, comprehensive management level, market influence and reputation of Yinfa would be further improved because NBEE is more suitable for most local enterprises in Ningbo in terms of its degree of intervention as an intermediary, requirements on information disclosure and other aspects. The growth in NBEE will lay a solid foundation for listing of Yinfa in NEEQ and IPO in future.

When Wang Yong was 11 years old, he dropped out of school to help his parents plant and pickle potherb mustard and sell pickled potherb mustard. Relying on this skill, he became a provincial intangible cultural heritage inheritor of pickled potherb mustard "Xian Ji" and developed Yinfa into a leading agricultural enterprise in Ningbo. However, the relatively low production and industry thresholds restricted the growth and development of Yinfa. Later, his daughter and son-in-law who returned from studying abroad brought some new ideas to the corporate development. In response to the rural revitalization strategy of China, they founded Spark Agricultural Incubator Platform to introduce innovation through the construction of such an agricultural science & technology incubator.

2. Internal Resources of Company

(1) Physical Resources

With years' technical development and marketing, Yinfa has developed into a comprehensive food processing enterprise integrating R&D, planting, processing and marketing of food. Its products are mainly divided into five categories: pickles, seasonings, starch products, cereal products, and canned food. The company's factory covers an area of 56 acres, with a factory area of 30000 square meters. It has a 2000 acre snow planting base and a series of complete pickled vegetable production lines in the workshop. At present, Yinfa has idle plant, workshop, equipment and other resources,

(2) Financial Resources

The financial resources are mainly from the capital contribution made by the founders at the inception of the company and the outstanding sales performance among similar products for many years. In 2018, the annual production of agricultural products of Yinfa reached CNY 30 million, of which that from potherb mustard and preserved vegetables accounted for 70%. Yinfa took lead in this market segment.

(3) Technical Resources

Pickled potherb mustard is one of the main products of Yinfa. Its raw material needs undergo scientific seed selection, timely planting, rational fertilization, fine harvesting, and relies on fertile soil, suitable climate and the traditional pickling process inherited for many years, in which R&D personnel have carried out continuous research, accumulation, improvement and upgrade of the pickling procss. Now with the changes of the times, consumers' taste might change while enjoying the local food. On one hand, Yinfa maintained the original authentic taste with the traditional pickling processes, and on the other hand, Yinfa also made improvements and innovations to the traditional processes.

(4) Corporate Culture and Image

As a inheritor of the intangible cultural heritage program "Qiu Ai Potherb Mustard Pickling Skills", Yinfa has its unique corporate culture. It takes "making fine food with strong local features to make it everlasting" as its mission, and regards "quality-oriented, agile action, lean operation, cherishing the value of labor and diligence" as its business philosophy. Wang Yong applied for Intangible Cultural Heritage for his pickling process and invested to build a potherb mustard museum when he found that people have certain bias and misunderstanding in pickled food. In this way, he hoped the culture of pickled potherb mustard could be promoted and the pickling process could be inherited. Furthermore, he wanted to tell people that scientifically pickled food is not harmful to health as they thought, instead, it was delicious and healthy. Now the museum has become a unique cultural symbol of Yinfa. Relying on this, Yinfa receives a large number of partners or visitors each year, organizes the Potherb Mustard cultural festival and invites citizens to participate, and also organizes intangible cultural heritage activities with the government to promote the culture of pickled potherb mustard. All of these have imperceptibly promoted the development of Yinfa.

(5) Human Resources

At present, Yinfa has a total of 120 employees, including 13 managers, 5 technicians and 102 workers. Yinfa is lack of professional agricultural technicians, which has constrained further technological innovation of the company in recent years. In the survey of age distribution of the employees of Yinfa, it is found that the age distribution is relatively balanced, most of which are in the age of 30-50 years old. In particular, the technicians are all in the age of 30-40, 84.6% of management personnel are in the age of 30-40, and 55% workers are between 40 and 50 years old. There is no employee of 20-30 years old.

3. Niche Strategy with Potherb Mustard as the Core

Yinfa adheres to the concepts of healthy and green food and traditional processing. Its main products are pickled potherb mustard, preserved vegetables and prawn crackers. Pickled potherb mustard and preserved vegetables are mainly supplied to the central kitchens of catering industry, such as fast food restaurants, to be as ingredients for cooking. As potherb mustard is just a local specialty of Ningbo, the target market is limited and the target consumer are mostly in Jiangsu, Zhejiang and Shanghai. The sales of potherb mustard in other regions is relatively small. Moreover the whole market of pickles is gradually shrinking due to the emergence of alternatives such as dried radish, and the concern about the health problems brought by pickled products. Therefore based on the niche strategy, Yinfa decided to develop potherb mustard and preserved vegetables products in depth and started to offer seasoning products based on the potherb mustard and preserved vegetables. With such seasoning products, the consumers need only to add seasoning in their cooking to get the authentic flavor of specialty dishes. The advantage of seasoning products is simple and convenient. At present, Yinfa offers five categories of seasoning products: fried pork and dried radish, boiled fish and pickled Chinese cabbage, steamed fish and snow vegetable, braised meat and preserved vegetables (osmanthus crystal sugar) and braised meat and preserved vegetables (delicious and salty).

The advantages of Yinfa's pickled potherb mustard are the quality of raw materials and the cultural features of Yinfa. The pickled potherb mustard of Yinfa is all made with high-quality potherb mustard planted in strict accordance with the requirements. The market feedback is better. In addition, Yinfa has promoted the culture of potherb mustard, established a museum, and formed its unique cultural resources.

4. Platform Strategy with Spark Agricultural Incubator Platform

Xingchuang Tiandi is a manifestation of crowdsourcing space at the grassroots level in rural areas, and it is a inheritance and promotion of the Spark Plan. In short, Xingchuang Tiandi is a platform for agricultural science and technology innovation and entrepreneurship, serving the land with innovation and entrepreneurship. It is not only a "school" for new professional farmers but also a "cradle" for innovative agricultural entrepreneurs. It is an important component of the rural science and technology innovation and entrepreneurship service system and an important measure to promote the system of science and technology special envoys. Xingchuang Tiandi provides a good environment for rural innovation and entrepreneurship, lowers the threshold for entrepreneurship, and reduces entrepreneurial risks. Compared to the Spark Plan, Xingchuang Tiandi has further improved its service targets, content, and methods, shifting from serving traditional agriculture and farmers to serving modern agriculture and new professional farmers; Transforming from demonstrating and promoting practical technologies that are short, flat, and fast to transferring and transforming agricultural high-tech that is high, new, and unique; Transforming from "technology research and development management" to "innovative services"; Transitioning from the addition of "exporting one person and getting rich" to the multiplication of "one person starting a business and getting rich"; Transforming from the goal of promoting rural industrialization to the goal of promoting the integration of primary, secondary, and tertiary industries in rural areas, as well as the development of industry, city, town, and village integration. As an important component of the rural science and technology innovation service system with enterprises as the main body and market orientation, Xingchuang Tiandi provides comprehensive services for agricultural and rural innovation and entrepreneurship, and constructs an innovation and entrepreneurship incubation service chain of "entrepreneurship nursery+incubator+accelerator". In addition to delving deeper into professional fields, the company entered the second batch of recommended filing lists for Xingchuang Tiandi published by the Ministry of Science and Technology in 2017, and began exploring agricultural incubation.

Yinfa has assigned special management personnel for the service platform and with such a platform, Yinfa is looking forward to finding a new profitability mode, for example, leasing its idle workshops and sites to the start-ups in the service center park and providing processing and packaging design and other services for them. Only in this way, Yinfa may change its traditional management mode which just pursues increase of product sales and then increase its competitive advantages. Such a platform strategy is conductive to Yinfa because the rent of its canteen, dormitory building and site is relatively low and it has idle workshops, equipment and sites. In addition, Yinha has also introduced Ningbo Yinzhou District Agricultural Cooperatives to integrate with the technical platform, trading platform and service platform of "Spark Agricultural Incubator Platform" to provide more technical guidance, which means that the start-ups can complete product production, processing and packaging at lower prices and get technical guide through the platform introduced by Yinfa, thus producing better products at lower costs. Also through the service platform, Yinfa can attract various resources and strength to promote the transformation of its agricultural production organization mode to be intensive and efficient, realize optimal resources allocation, and exploit the value of idle equipment and site, ultimately promoting the agricultural transformation and upgrading and improving its competitive advantage. All of this will contribute to the long-term development of Yinfa. However, the platform has not realized the desirable results because Yinfa is located in a remote place. Moreover, although Yinfa wishes to introduce more agricultural product enterprises, the companies that are currently introduced are mainly Chinese medicine health care and horticultural enterprises.

Should Yinfa select in-depth development to extend the value chain of potherb mustard, or platform-based and diversified strategy to exploit more market space? It is hard to decide. At present, Yinfa chooses to implement both. But can such a situation sustain in the long run? Which field should the company's limited resources be invested in to make Yinfa transform successfully? This is an important issue in front of the decision-makers of Yinfa.

Questions:

【Case 4】 1. What important influence that the internal environment of Yinfa made when it selects development strategy?

2.What tangible and intangible resources does Yinfa have?

3.Which resources and capabilities of Yinfa can help it build its core competitiveness? Use VRIO model to identify the advantages and disadvantages of internal resources and capabilities of an enterprise.

Tips for answering the questions:

1. This question is about the importance of internal environment analysis. If a company wants to develop and retain its competitive advantages, it must obtain, bundle and make use of various resources. The analysis from the internal environment of the enterprise is to determine how to realize the exertion and strengthening of competitive advantages and create greater value for customers through the allocation and integration of existing and limited resources.

2. Understand the definition and connotation of tangible resources and intangible resources. Tangible resources refer to assets that can be directly measured by value indicators or monetary indicators, have physical form or can be seen and clearly defined in quantity. Intangible resources refer to assets that can create benefits for the organization, but do not have independent physical form.

3. Core competence refers to the force of elements that are in the core position and can enable an organization to surpass its competitors and obtain greater profits. There are four elements for internal resources that can help enterprises obtain core competitiveness: value, rarity, inimitability and organization.

Case 5

Competitive Strategy of Fenbi (A Platform for Civil Servant Examination Training)

Key points:

Porter's Five Forces Model, business resource and competency analysis, focus and differentiation strategies

Case Purpose:

This case is intended to strengthen the students' understanding and application of strategy tools such as macro environment analysis, resources analysis, core competitiveness analysis and Porter's Five Forces model, and help the students to understand the basic form and conditions of application of the competitive strategy.

Case Description:

1. Emergence of Fenbi

In 2013, Zhang Xiaolong took over the position of CEO of Beijing Fenbi Blue Sky Technology Co., Ltd. (hereinafter referred to as Fenbi), and Fenbi began to provide online training of civil servant examination on the platform. From 2013 to 2014, the operating revenue from civil servant examination training reached CNY 5 million, of which that from the various training courses was CNY 0.5 million ~ 0.6 million.

Onerous training courses and high requirements on quality lead to heavy workload, but Zhang Xiaolong did not want to compromise on the quality. In 2014, the number of civil servant examination training members of Fenbi was reduced to three, in which case, Zhang Xiaolong's team only held one training course. What types of training courses should be held? It was always the concern of Zhang Xiaolong's team. Based on the trainees' demands, Zhang finally chose to provide a integrated course. Then the next issue was pricing. At that time, the price of offline civil servant exam training was relatively expensive.

Zhang believed that its online training course must be outstanding to beat the offline civil servant exam training competitors. The price of its online training must be much lower than the market price. As the price of Huatu was about CNY 2,000, Zhang Xiaolong's team set its price to CNY 680. After setting the price, the concern of Zhang Xiaolong's team was that if it was too high and exceeded the trainees' expectation, the trainees were reluctant to pay, and if it was too low, the trainees might concern about the quality. Finally, the integrated course realized excellent sales.

In 2015, the sales of the civil servant examination training integrated course of Fenbi maintained a rapid growth. Then some members of the team proposed to add other courses to get more profit? Some trainees also hoped Fenbi could provide sprint course and Q&A course. Therefore, Zhang launched sprint course at a rate of CNY 90, which was sold separately but offered to the trainees of the integrated course for free. In the first half of 2015, Fenbi sold out 10000 sprint courses with an operating income of CNY 1 million, of which the profit reached more than CNY 0.9 million. The sprint course increased the profit, but in the long run, some problems also arose. The sales of the integrated course declined due to sales of the sprint course, and probability of failing the exam also increased because some trainees only participated in the sprint course. It affected the reputation of Fenbi. Furthermore, the service process for the sprint course was not as good as the integrated course. Considering these reasons, Zhang Xiaolong's team resolutely gave up the sprint course.

From then on, Zhang Xiaolong's team focused on the integrated course. They actively improved the products according to the feedback of trainees. In 2015 and 2016, Fenbi achieved satisfactory performance in the civil servant exam training market. Many pepole suggested Zhang to increase the price of the integrated course, but Zhang refused. Instead, he continued to focus on the continual optimization of products.

At the inception, they only provided online education services, but later the students requested them to provide printed teaching materials for the online courses. Zhang

Case 5 Competitive Strategy of Fenbi (A Platform for Civil Servant Examination Training) | 153

Xiaolong's team decided to publish books of the teaching materials. They chose the best paper and even additional additives to protect the eyesight of students. In order to enhance the style of the books, they chose the straight stitching binding method. Besides, they engaged a special design studio to carry out the design of cover and the layout of text to improve the visual comfort of trainees. All these improvement work inevitably led to an increase in cost. Zhang Xiaolong's team decided to increase by CNY 200. At that time, Zhang was afraid that the price increase would affect sales. Fortunately, that did not affect the enthusiasm of the students significantly. In 2017, the operating revenue exceeded CNY 100 million, and the number of fixed trainees exceeded 300,000. In 2022, Fenbi achieved a revenue of CNY 2.81 billion and a gross profit of CNY 1.37 billion, an increase of 62.4% year-on-year from CNY 840 million in 2021. During the same period, the gross profit margin increased rapidly from 24.5% to 48.6%.

2. Iteration and Updating of Fenbi

Fenbi believed that education itself needed to be iteratively updated, especially for Fenbi that offered services in the later stages. In order to maintain competition of products, Fenbi made innovations in the following aspects:

(1) Iteration of employees

For the famous teachers who advocated personality, Fenbi invited them to join the team and improved their teamwork skills. Even for other supporting positions, Fenbi also attached great importance in the recruiting. For example the customer service employees are mostly fresh graduates. Fenbi provided work skills training for newcomers and required the employees to think independently. Fenbi required the customer service department to draft a report every year to summarize the issues reflected by the trainees in the year and propose their solutions.

(2) Product evolution

At present, high product barriers have been established by the books of Fenbi. For example, through the App, the most important part in the product evolution, the trainees can import the job list they have applied for into the platform to view the rankings.

(3) Service upgrade

Initially Fenbi offered learning materials after the students paid the tuition, later Fenbi established acommunication group in which the head teacher would send the relevant exam materials to the students. In order to improve the enthusiasm of trainees, Fenbi took a series of measures such as knowledge evaluation and exam before entering the group, and making audios and videos for boring text materials, etc.

Based on trainee feedback, Fenbi completed its own iteration and update to provide meticulous and thoughtful services to the students. Instead of expensive advertising, Fenbi spent a lot on product research and development to serve core users. It was well recognized by the trainees. In 2018, the number of applicants for the national civil servant examination reached a record high but the pass rate decreased year by year. Competition became fiercer and the civil servant examination training market had a bright future. Applicants preferred to select online training because it could not only protect their personal privacy, but also save the time for commuting, especially for the applicants in the third- and fourth-tier cities who were ignored by offline civil servant examination institutions. Fenbi can meet the needs of them.

At the inception, Fenbi made efforts to attract attention and build its brand by means of the question bank and intelligent modification system. After that, it conducted online live streaming, book sale, and offline interview courses. The team conducted in-depth research on the examination questions, evaluated the students' learning level by AI technology, and based on this, designed personalized questions and providing students with one-to-one Q&A course. The team actively collected feedback to update the question bank, and invited famous teachers to join the team to obtain professional analysis of exam questions. At the same time, it also provided simulated exam environment based on the real exam questions, increased the time limit for exam and intelligent correction to get true experience. In addition, Fenbi provided learning materials such as question banks, materials, videos, and standardized courses and content to complete the channelization transformation.

The profit of Fenbi, although not high, was maintained at a relatively reasonable level. Fenbi continued to add content, products and services. The software version was updated more than 20 times a year, and details such as background services were also continuously optimized. All of these have driven Fenbi to gradually become the leader of the online civil servant examination training market.

3. Strategic Choice under Fierce Competition

The huge online civil servant examination training market attracted numerous copycats. They offered integrated course at a rate of CNY 590, as compared with Fenbi's integrated course of CNY 680. But they have gradually disappeared over time.

The competitors of Fenbi were not the peer online civil servant examination training institutions, but the piracy. In order to compete with the terrible pirates, Fenbi allowed its course to be played repeatedly. In addition, Fenbi offered more materials and workbooks, online Q&A, and allowed the trainees to change the play speed of course, pause the play, and take notes on the interface. Through continuous optimization of its products, Fenbi improved the product barrier to a level that is unattainable for the pirates.

With the emergence of the education live stream industry, the number of registered trainees of the online platforms such as Zhonggong and Huatu increased significantly. In particular, Huatu invested to acquire 30% shares of an online civil servant examination training company. In 2018, Zhonggong was listed on the A-share market and Huatu proposed to be listed on Hong Kong Main Board in the form of H shares and 60% of the raised funds was planned to be used for offline business expansion and network construction.

The success of Fenbi in the training and education industry is inseparable from the internet, artificial intelligence and big data technologies. These technologies brought great benefits to Fenbi, but also were applied by many potential competitors. The core team had made intense discussions on how to make the competitive strategy. Some executives believed that the rapid rise of Fenbi showed that focusing on core products and core trainees was a practical and feasible route that was proved proper by the market. Although some competitors may copy the model of Fenbi, Fenbi could expand its advantages together with the competitors as long as it insisted on the existing model. It was expected that in the coming years, the civil servant examination training market would maintain a steady upward trend, and the strategy of focusing on core products and continuously optimizing services would not only enable Fenbi to maintain steady growth, but also avoid many potential risks. However, other executives believed that as compared with offline civil servant examination training organizations, the advantage of Fenbi was that it was based on the platform, and a company could only maintain sustainable development by giving full play to its own advantages. Fenbi had made considerable success in the civil servant examination training market, but this market is only a relatively small market in the entire training market. Fenbi will lose development opportunities if it is self-satisfied. In the long run, Fenbi should, while retaining the existing operation mode, turn its focus of business from the civil servant examination training to other vocational examination training, ultimately realizing overall development. However, abandoning a safe route and turning to a relatively unfamiliar field will also bring great risks.

【Case 5】

Questions:

(1) As compared with other civil servant examination training organizations, what is the advantages of Fenbi in internal resources and capabilities?

(2) What competitive strategy has Fenbi taken to successfully and quickly seize the online civil servant examination training market? Explain the reasons for such strategies?

(3) What do you think opportunities and threats are there in the civil servant examination training market?

(4) What strategies Fenbi shall make confronted with its competitors?

Tips for answering the questions:

1. The internal resources and capabilities of an enterprise can help the enterprise gain competitive advantage. In this topic, the internal core resources and capabilities of Fenbi can be analyzed and discovered from the perspective of the value chain. For example, the R&D of the integrated course, the R&D of the APP, the artificial intelligence evaluation, and the intelligent correction all reflect the R&D ability of Fenbi. Furthermore, it includes knowledge evaluation before entering the group, audio and video making for text materials, software version updating for more than 20 times a year, and constant optimization of background services, etc.

2. Porter put forward three basic competitive strategies: cost leadership strategy, differentiation strategy and centralization strategy. Cost leadership strategy is to take a whole set of actions to provide customers with acceptable products or services with certain characteristics at a cost lower than that of competitors. Differentiation strategy refers to a series of actions to produce products or provide services in a differentiated way that customers think is important. The centralization strategy is to focus on a specific customer group, a segment of a product series or a regional market. Students can analyze what kind of competition strategy Fenbi adopted according to its customer characteristics, product content, etc.

3. This topic examines the analysis of the external environment of the enterprise. Students shall identify opportunities and threats in the external environment from the perspective of the macro environment, industrial environment and competitive environment in combination with the description of the competitive situation in the case.

4. The case gives two ideas: one is to continue to focus on the civil servants examination training business, and the other is to expand to other vocational examination fields. It

can be analyzed from the perspective of focusing on the strengths and weaknesses of the strategy, or based on the analysis of the internal and external environment. Students may use the SWOT analysis (strengths, weaknesses, opportunities, threats) to give suggestions on strategic decisions.

Case 6

Dynamic Competition Among Three Companies on Sodium Methoxide

Key points:

Competitor analysis; Dynamic competition; Awareness-Motivation-Capability (AMC) model

Case Purpose:

This case helps students understand the use of the AMC model and the logic behind dynamic competition through introducing the competition inter-action of three companies on sodium methoxide in multiple markets.

Case Description:

1. Operations of Three Chemical Companies on Sodium Methoxide

Ningbo Zhetie Jiangning Chemical Co., Ltd. (hereinafter referred to as Jiangning Chemical), established in June 2007 with a registered capital of CNY 700 million, is a high-tech company in Ningbo and a subsidiary of Zhejiang Transportation Investment Group Co., Ltd. Jiangning Chemical is mainly engaged in the development, production, sales and technical service of chemicals, with maleic anhydride and sodium methoxide as major products. The sales territory covers more than ten provinces and municipalities at home and Europe, America and Southeast Asia in abroad market.

Anhui Jinbang Pharmaceutical Chemical Co., Ltd. (hereinafter referred to as Anhui JB) founded in 1995, the company was restructured as a private enterprise in 2001. It is a provincial-level "contract abiding and trustworthy enterprise" with AAA level bank credit and self operated import and export rights. Anhui Jinbang is committed to the development and production of fine chemicals, pharmaceutical intermediates, biochemical reagents, and food additives. Its leading products include sodium methoxide (powder and solution), ether, sodium ethanol (powder and solution), sodium tert butanol, etc. At present, Anhui Jinbang has become a powerful methanol sodium production enterprise. Anhui Jinbang attaches great importance to the improvement of product quality and service quality, strives to effectively integrate technology with various resources, continuously improve product technology and quality, and meet the diverse needs of users to the greatest extent. The company has passed a series of certifications such as ISO9001 quality system. Anhui Jinbang's products are highly trusted by domestic and foreign users, enjoying a high reputation. The domestic market share has been increasing year by year, and they have been exported to many countries and regions in Europe, Asia, and America for many consecutive years.

Henan Shenghongfeng Chemical Co., Ltd., (hereinafter referred to as Henan SHF) was established in 2012. Located in the national fine chemical industrial area, the company covers an area of 60,000 square meters with an annual output of 160,000 tons of sodium methoxide. It is a comprehensive chemical enterprise capable of research, production and sales. The company currently has six sets of liquid methanol sodium equipment, with an annual production of 210000 tons of liquid methanol sodium and methanol; Two sets of solid methanol sodium equipment, with an annual output of 20000 tons of high-purity solid methanol sodium.

The market scope of sodium methoxide products of these three companies are generally overlapped, namely in Zhejiang, Jiangxi, Jiangsu, Fujian and Southeast Asian countries. From the perspective of capacity scale and strength, Anhui JB has a registered capital of CNY 30 million. It has been in the industry for a long time, and is the maker of the industry standard. The quality and service reputation of sodium methoxide are very good. Henan SHF has a registered capital of CNY 10 million. Its current production capacity is the largest in Asia and its market is all over the world. The production capacity of Jiangning Chemical is 28,000 tons, with a strong growth momentum. In terms of port resources, Anhui JB is close to Nanjing Port, Henan SHF is close to Lianyungang, and Jiangning

Chemical is close to Ningbo Port. Therefore, the three companies are equal in downstream market, resources, size and strength, and they are direct competitors.

2. Analysis on Situation in Dynamic Competition

This part analyzes a series of competitions between Jiangning Chemical and Anhui JB and Henan SHF from 2010 to 2020. Three companies have took many actions such as competing in domestic regional markets, competing by improving product quality and changing status, making strategic shifts in markets, and competing in foreign markets. Companies demonstrated their advantages in resources and capabilities during the competition, which is worth studying and discussing. Types used to distinguish their various competitive behaviors during this period are as follows.

(1) Aggressive Behaviors

Companies usually take aggressive behaviors in order to maintain their advantages continuously in the market competition. Based on the different degrees of AMC's three drivers, aggressive behaviors can be divided into six types: Awareness (Sensitive), Awareness (Insensitive), Motivation (Strong), Motivation (Weak), Capability (High), Capability (Low). Aggressive strategies for Awareness (Sensitive) include competitive advertising, price reduction with extensive advertising, and publicly-announced growth target setting. Aggressive strategies for Awareness (Insensitive) are generally internal improvement, such as higher quality of products and services, greater operational efficiency, structural mergers and reorganizations, etc. Aggressive strategies for Motivation (Strong), with clear sense of aggression, use advantages of resources to attack opponents in their core or main markets, or launch direct attack and seize markets with huge potential and room for growth. Focusing on sharing, aggressive strategies for Motivation (Weak) consist of attacking opponents in non-core markets or claiming a position in the market where the opponent has established a strong and stable position. Aggressive strategies for Capability (High) requires companies having proprietary technologies or resources that are hardly available to their opponents, making joint actions with external participants when necessary, and provides a relatively complete mechanism that supports the coordination among functional departments, etc. Aggressive strategies for Capability (Weak) includes price reduction, advertising war, promotion and other concessions.

(2) Reactive Behaviors

Generally, reactive behaviors in response to aggression are divided into four categories: Neglect, Acceptance, Abandonment and Retaliation. Companies choose to ignore competitor threats when they are little and follow the original strategy without taking any action. When a company only gains parts of market share, while more competitors bring an increasing market demand, or competitive behaviors would hurt the interests of both parties at different levels, the company chooses to accept new competitors. Abandonment is often due to the inability to resist the attacks by the advantage of the attacker. Abandonment means lower losses. The retaliation requires that the initiator has or will have competitive advantages, takes advantage to push competitors to adopt stronger expansion strategies and prevent competitors from entering the market or performing further aggressive behaviors.

3. Process and Analysis of Dynamic Competition

Table 6-1 shows the dynamic competition process of the three companies from 2010 to 2020 based on the AMC model:

Case 6 Dynamic Competition Among Three Companies on Sodium Methoxide | 165

Table 6–1 Dynamic Competition Process of the Three Companies from 2010 to 2020 Based on the AMC Model

Competition Phase	Aggressor's Behaviors	Reactor	Reactor's AMC			Reactive Behaviors	Outcome
			Awareness	Motivation	Capability		
Phase I	Jiangning Chemical expanded its sodium methoxide production and entered the market with lower prices	Anhui JB	Anhui JB was aware of Jiangning Chemical's business model and marketing strategies	Since the production cost was higher than that of Jiangning Chemical, Anhui JB expanded the business to other markets to avoid vicious competition	Anhui JB was able to select high-quality clients in its abundant customers resources	Acceptance	Jiangning Chemical entered the markets in Zhejiang, Jiangxi, Anhui, Jiangsu, etc. The market in Zhejiang took up about 40%
	Anhui JB increased the production load of solid sodium methoxide and expanded the high-end pharmaceutical market that is profitable	Jiangning Chemical	Jiangning Chemical was aware of information about production process and investment on solid sodium methoxide	Since the production of for solid sodium methoxide had high technical requirements, Jiangning Chemical didn't have the capability at the time being	Jiangning Chemical was unfamiliar with the production technology of solid sodium methoxide	Neglect	Anhui JB gained almost all clients in East China for solid sodium methoxide
	Jiangning Chemical carried out technical transformation, increased production to lower its cost, improved product quality, and started a price war against competitors	Anhui JB	Anhui JB was aware of Jiangning Chemica's expansion plan, sales area and major downstream industries	Anhui JB cracked down Jiangning Chemical by price cut to sustain its market share in the regions with advantages on hands	Anhui JB had various products, packaging and sales channels	Retaliation	Jiangning Chemical successfully snatched Anhui JB's market in Zhejiang, Jiangxi and Fujian.

continued

Competition Phase	Aggressor's Behaviors	Reactor	Reactor's AMC			Reactive Behaviors	Outcome
			Awareness	Motivation	Capability		
	Anhui JB expanded business to overseas markets	Jiangning Chemical	Jiangning Chemical focused on surrounding regional markets, insensitive to overseas markets	Jiangning Chemical sustained a balance between production and sales, with no interest in targeting new markets	Jiangning Chemical's marketing team fell short of ability in overseas market	Abandonment	Anhui JB expanded business to overseas markets and gained many clients and high profits
	Anhui JB improved product quality and took the lead in establishing industry standards	Jiangning Chemical	Jiangning Chemical was aware of qualifications of pilot companies to establish industry standards	Jiangning Chemical seized the opportunity as pilot company to establish industry standards for greater influence	Jiangning Chemical had experience in establishing national and industry standards on other products	Retaliation	Anhui JB took the lead in establishing industry standards 2014 and built a strong brand image
	Anhui JB retained domestic core clients with high profitability and made strides into Southeast Asia	Jiangning Chemical	Jiangning Chemical was insensitive to overseas market	Developing overseas markets came with high cost and Jiangning Chemical was satisfied with its profits in domestic market	Jiangning Chemical didn't have sufficient production to develop overseas markets	Abandonment	Anhui JB had a significant increase in export volume with high profits
	Jiangning Chemical carried out technical transformation and production expansion to fill the regional market gap	Anhui JB	Anhui JB showed little interest in the competitive domestic market with low price	Biodiesel overseas markets is a blue ocean market with high profit	Anhui JB didn't have extra products to compete in the domestic sales	Neglect	Jiangning Chemical further increased its market share in the surrounding area

Case 6 Dynamic Competition Among Three Companies on Sodium Methoxide | 167

continued

Competition Phase	Aggressor's Behaviors	Reactor's AMC				Reactive Behaviors	Outcome
		Reactor	Awareness	Motivation	Capability		
	Henan SHF expanded its capacity to fill the gap in the domestic surrounding market, and quickly entered the fast-growing biodiesel market in Southeast Asia	Jiangning Chemical	Jiangning Chemical was insensitive to overseas market	Developing overseas markets came with high cost and Jiangning Chemical was satisfied with its profits in domestic market	Jiangning Chemical sustained a balance between production and sales, with no interest in targeting new markets	Abandonment	Henan SHF successfully developed biodiesel market in Southeast Asia
		Anhui JB	Anhui JB was aware of Henan SHF's FOB price, customers and others	Anhui JB also lowered export price to maintain its market share in Southeast Asia	Anhui JB was well-known in the Southeast Asian market, familiar with business processes	Retaliation	
Phase II	Anhui JB gave up parts of its domestic market and further increased its overseas markets share	Jiangning Chemical	Jiangning Chemical was insensitive to overseas market	Developing overseas markets came with high cost and Jiangning Chemical was satisfied with its profits in domestic market	Jiangning Chemical sustained a balance between production and sales, with no interest in targeting abroad markets	Abandonment	Anhui JB compressed Henan SHF's share of biodiesel market in Southeast Asia
		Henan SHF	Henan SHF paid attention to feedback from downstream clients and customs export data	Henan SHF decreased prices and worked with export intermediaries to develop new channels	Henan SHF had sufficient capacity and large cost advantage, with no fear of price war	Retaliation	

continued

Competi-tion Phase	Aggressor's Behaviors	Reactor's AMC					Reactive Behaviors	Outcome
		Reactor	Awareness	Motivation	Capability		
	Jiangning Chemical witnessed a fast-shrinking markets in the surrounding area and developed overseas markets	Henan SHF	Henan SHF paid attention to feedback from downstream clients and customs export data	Henan SHF decreased export prices to maintain market share in Southeast Asia	Henan SHF had certain reputation in overseas markets with a large cost advantage	Retaliation	Jiangning Chemical entered the Southeast Asian market but with a small share
		Anhui JB	Anhui JB paid attention to feedback from downstream clients and customs export data	Anhui JB maintains certain market shares in Southeast Asia. The excess capacity was shifted to solid products sold to high-end pharmaceutical clients with relatively high profitability	Anhui JB had high reputation in overseas markets, good customer relationship, various product structure and wide channels	Acceptance	
	Jiangning Chemical relocated its plant, expanded the capacity, and further reduced production cost. It also increased the export volume to Southeast Asia and neighboring markets to increase its share in overseas markets	Henan SHF	Henan SHF forecasted which sales area Jiangning Chemical would enter and at what price	Henan SHF actively prepared for price war and was ready to decrease prices	Henan SHF had low cost, good customer relationship, and strong market competitiveness	Retaliation	Jiangning Chemical increased share of Southeast Asia market
		Anhui JB	Anhui JB forecasted which sales area Jiangning Chemical would enter and at what price	Anhui JB actively prepared for price war and was ready to decrease prices	Anhui JB had high costs in production and transportation and insufficient capability for head-on competition	Retaliation	

Case 6 Dynamic Competition Among Three Companies on Sodium Methoxide | 169

continued

Competition Phase	Aggressor's Behaviors	Reactor	Awareness	Motivation	Capability	Reactive Behaviors	Outcome
	Henan SHF expanded its capacity to target market shares owned by other companies at home and abroad, and designed the equipment for the production of solid sodium methoxide to enter the high-end pharmaceutical market	Anhui JB	Anhui JB forecasted Henan SHF's sales territory, timing and price	Anhui JB prepared for price wars	Anhui JB market had operated for a long time and received a high level of trust from clients.	Retaliation	Henan SHF took parts of domestic and global market share from Anhui JB and Jiangning Chemical, and made layout on domestic high-end pharmaceutical market
		Jiangning Chemical	Jiangning Chemical forecasted Henan SHF's sales territory, timing and price	Jiangning Chemical prepared for price wars	Jiangning Chemical had advantages in domestic regional markets for liquid products, with low export cost and in its location close to the Port of Ningbo.	Retaliation/Partial Acceptance	
	Anhui JB expanded into South American, African and other overseas markets	Jiangning Chemical	Jiangning Chemical paid close attention to South American, African and other overseas markets for the right timing of its entrance	Jiangning Chemical expanded overseas client base and gained high profits from new market entry	Jiangning Chemical's export department accumulated experience. The company is close to the Port of Ningbo with low transportation costs.	Acceptance	Anhui JB expanded into South American and African markets with sales pressure eased
		Henan SHF	Henan SHF focused on the fast-growing biodiesel market in Southeast Asia, insensitive to other international markets	Southeast Asia's biodiesel market growing fast, Henan SHF must sustain its market share	Henan SHF didn't have sufficient ability to develop new markets	Neglect	

continued

Competition Phase	Aggressor's Behaviors	Reactor	Reactor's AMC			Reactive Behaviors	Outcome
			Awareness	Motivation	Capability		
	Henan SHF had another production capacity expansion to increase its market share at home and abroad, striving to be a leading manufacturer in Asia.	Anhui JB	Anhui JB forecasted Henan SHF's sales territory, timing and price and was aware of Henan SHF's actual capacity after expansion	Anhui JB traded its biodiesel market share for Henan's share in the domestic high-end pharmaceutical market. It strove to be the biggest manufacturer in Asia and put effort in building its brand	Anhui JB had greater influence in the overseas markets and was well-known in the domestic market. It's easier for Anhui JB to increase its share of high-end market	Retaliation	With increasing market share of overseas biodiesel market, Henan SHF became the biggest manufacturer of sodium methoxide in Asia with higher visibility of the company and its products
		Jiangning Chemical	Jiangning Chemical forecasted Henan SHF's sales territory, timing and price	Jiangning Chemical actively prepared for price wars in overseas biodiesel markets	Jiangning Chemical had an advantage in production costs with lower export costs due to its location close to the Port of Ningbo	Retaliation	
	Jiangning Chemical repositioned itself in the market to develop the high-end pharmaceutical market in the surrounding region	Anhui JB	Anhui JB paid attention to when Jiangning Chemical would enter the high-end pharmaceutical market	Anhui JB leveraged advantages long accumulated in its brand to gain quality customers and sustain its market share	Anhui JB entered the market early with many loyal customers and a good brand image.	Retaliation	Jiangning Chemical successfully entered the surrounding high-end pharmaceutical market and grasped some shares
		Henan SHF	Henan SHF paid attention to when Anhui JB would enter the high-end pharmaceutical market	Henan SHF prepared for price wars	Henan SHF had lower production costs in general with advantages in its prices and high influence as the biggest manufacturer.	Retaliation	

continued

Competi-tion Phase	Aggressor's Behaviors	Reactor's AMC					Reactive Behaviors	Outcome
		Reactor	Awareness	Motivation	Capability		
	Anhui JB further expanded its production to compete for biodiesel markets and domestic mass market and reclaimed its position as a leading manufacturer in Asia.	Jiangning Chemical	Jiangning Chemical forecasted which markets Anhui JB would enter and at what time and what price	Jiangning Chemical prepared for price wars	Jiangning Chemical had the advantage in production costs and export costs, high quality and good reputation.	Retaliation	
		Henan SHF	Henan SHF forecasted which markets Anhui JB would enter and at what time and what price, and was aware of Anhui JB's newly-added capacity	Henan SHF prepared for price wars and made sufficient preparation to compete with Anhui JB for its leading position as the biggest manufacturer in Asia	Henan SHF had lower production costs in general with a large price advantage and great reputation in the domestic and overseas markets	Retaliation	Anhui JB increased its biodiesel market share and reclaimed its position as the biggest manufacturer in Asia

Through the description of the dynamic competition of the three companies, Anhui JB launched attacks with high quality and strong capability, especially good at developing new markets and fields. But it didn't launch counterattacks as frequently as Henan SHF, and its counterattacks were not fierce in the competitive mass markets. Henan SHF entered the market late, yet it kept launching strong attacks and counterattacks and fast grew its market and share. However, it didn't match Anhui JB in terms of the quality of attacks and the capability of counterattacks. Jiangning Chemical's attack and counterattack capabilities were weak before 2018; it then began to diversify its attacks and build stronger capabilities after 2018. The table also illustrates that Anhui JB adopted a differentiated competition strategy as a pioneer in the sales market. With the resources accumulated since it entered into the industry, Anhui JB kept improving product quality to build the brand to differentiate from its competitors. It continuously developed new markets to not have direct competition with other domestic competitors for high profits. Anhui JB had a disadvantage that it was expensive to develop new markets and the investment in sales was extremely high. Henan SHF implemented a cost advantage strategy, continuously taking cost advantage gained from its product portfolio to increase its market share. It gradually expanded sales business, which can promote the expansion of industry and production capacity, further reduce costs to form a virtuous circle. The obvious disadvantages were that Henan SHF was too persistent in increasing production capacity, leaving poor performance in sales, product quality and brand image. It largely used prices lower than average for high market share, but the profitability was not good though with a significant increase in its market share.

Questions:

【Case 6】

1. How do the three main factors of the AMC model affect in the case?

2. Please analyze the differences between aggressive behaviors and reactive behaviors of the three companies during the dynamic competition.

3. Please describe the differences in the strategies used by the three companies in the dynamic competition process.

4. What suggestions would you make for the three companies based on the above description of the dynamic competition?

Tips for answering the questions:

1. The AMC model is a predictive model to study, analyze, and understand attacks launched between competitors and responses after being attacked. The model attributes the core driving factors to the awareness of the other's behavior, the motivation of self reaction and the capability of self reaction. The three main factors can be interpreted from the micro and macro levels.

2. Based on the different degrees of AMC's three driving factors, aggressive behaviors can be divided into six types: Awareness (Sensitive), Awareness (Insensitive), Motivation (Strong), Motivation (Weak), Capability (High), Capability (Low); reactive behaviors can be divided into four types: Neglect, Accept, Abandon and Retaliate. The differences may be observed in the multiple attacks and reactions of the three companies.

3. The competitive strategy adopted by the companies can be judged according to the dynamic competitive behavior of the three companies and the characteristics of differentiation strategy and cost leadership strategy. The differentiation strategy is mainly reflected in the differentiation of products and services. The cost leadership strategy means that companies provide products with acceptable quality, but the cost is lower than that of competitors.

4. Analyze the awareness, motivation and capabilities of the three companies in the competition process, compare the advantages and disadvantages of the three companies in terms of resources and capabilities, and give strategic suggestions, either stick to the original strategy or propose new strategy.

Case 7

Hong Bang Tailors at a Crossroads of Diversification

Key points:

Importance of strategy; Corporate-level strategy; Diversification strategy

Case Purpose:

This case introduces the journey of diversification for apparel enterprises in Ningbo, with focus on the significant difference between the strategies developed by Ningbo Shanshan Co., Ltd. (hereinafter "Shanshan") and Youngor Group Co., Ltd. (hereinafter "Youngor"). The case is to help students understand the importance of strategic management and the concepts of diversification strategy. In particular, as strategy means diversification itself is not classified as good or bad, its management process is the key.

Case Description:

Ningbo tailors have long been making Western-style clothes. In the late Qing Dynasty and early Republic of China, Europeans arrived at the Port of Ningbo to explore Chinese market, and paid to local people for cloths making. They had red beards and wore very differently from the locals, so Ningbo tailors who made custom clothes for them were called "Hong Bang Tailors" (Hong means red, Bang means a cohort of people.). They made five "First" in the history of Chinese clothing, namely the first Western-style clothes, the first Zhongshan coat, the first Western-style clothing store, the first theoretical book on Western-style clothes and the first Western-style clothes school. Ningbo is home to many top brands like Romon, Taiping Bird, Tonlion, Progen, GXG, etc. Among others, the most famous ones are Li Rucheng's Youngor and Zheng Yonggang's Shanshan.

Turn left, or turn right?

Both being the leading companies in the apparel industry in China, Youngor and Shanshan march on different roads of industrial expansion. In 2002, Youngor formed a joint venture with Japanese Itochu and Nisshinbo to manage the upstream since the quality and purchase of apparel fabrics has a direct influence on the cloth textures, the manufacturing process, and the speed of consumer demand response. With this advantage, Youngor launched DP non-iron cotton shirts. They gained popularity in the market and have become the main shirt products with a monthly capacity of 400,000 pieces. Responding to global high requirements for ecofriendly and comfortable clothing fabrics, Youngor collaborated with the Military Equipment Research Institute of General Logistics Department of PLA and developed China-hemp fiber with improved breeding. As a result, the hemp products are soft, breathable, anti-mildew and deodorant. In 2007, Youngor invested CNY 48 million in Xishuangbanna Youngor Industrial Co., Ltd. (formerly as Hemp Industry Investment Holding Co.). In 2009, the world's first hemp fiber line, jointly invested by Youngor and Ningbo Yike Technology Industry Co Ltd., was put into operation with an annual production capacity of 5,000 tons, forming a guarantee for raw material supply. Although the hemp industry was still at a loss, Li Rucheng firmly believed that hemp has great business opportunities in the application of medicine, food, health products and other fields. In 2020, Youngor recorded revenue of CNY 5.75 billion, with profit reaching CNY 1.082 billion.

Unlike Youngor, Shanshan put major efforts into the downstream and adopted a multi-brand and internationalization strategy. Shanshan has established long-term collaborative relationships with world's famous apparel enterprises and institutions, such as Itochu, Forall, Renoma and the Fédération de la Haute Couture et de la Mode. Shanshan had more than 2,000 stores in China with a suit market share of 37.4% in its prime, but the number of stores decreased to 1,226 and market share shrank to 1.55% in 2018. In the same year, Shanshan spun off its apparel business to establish separately Shanshan Brand Operation Inc.

Fortunes Brought by Diversification

"Based on my experience, when an apparel company reaches an annual sale of CNY 50 million to CNY 100 million, there isn't much profit to earn due to the increasing inventory", said by an executive in the apparel industry. Then Youngor and Shanshan began to build other businesses, they started their journey of diversification.

In 1992, Youngor already had its first real estate company, Youngor Real Estate. But it didn't have rapid development until 2000. In 2000, Youngor launched the "East Lake Garden" project, marking the first entry in the real estate industry in Ningbo. Two years later, Youngor Real Estate achieved a revenue of CNY 534 million and started the implementation of the Yangtze River Delta Development Strategy. The company entered the Taizhou market in 2002, the Suzhou market in 2004, and the Hangzhou and Shaoxing markets in 2007. In 2010, the company reached a revenue of CNY 6.843 billion, surpassing apparel business revenue for the first time. The real estate business became the major business for Youngor. In 2020, its revenue reached CNY 5.071 billion with a total profit of CNY 2.014 billion. The real estate business contributed greatly to Youngor's performance as the apparel industry was hit by the COVID-19 pandemic. Besides the real estate business, Youngor also entered the financial investment to support diversification. Youngor took a stake in Bank of Ningbo in 1997 and invested CNY 320 million in CITIC Securities in 1999. Youngor made a series of equity investments afterwards and held shares of listed companies with market value worth of CNY 24 billion in its prime. Its operating income frequently fluctuated with the market. After two financial crises, Youngor gradually scaled down its financial investment business. According to the new financial instruments, Youngor had available-for-sale financial assets worth of CNY 19.6 billion to be reclassified as "financial assets measured at fair value through profit or loss".

When Youngor entered the real estate industry, Shanshan also created 100 multimillionaires with its apparel business. But the business was not very profitable and the inventory remained high. At the end of 1998, Shanshan's headquarters were relocated to Pudong, Shanghai. Despite missing a golden decade of real estate, Shanshan continued its efforts in science and technology and witnessed the start of the development of new energy industry.

In 2020, Shanshan achieved an income of CNY 6.915 billion in the lithium battery materials business and reached a year-on-year increase of 1.83%, with CNY 288 million as the net profit attributable to the listed company. Shanshan has become the world's largest integrated lithium battery materials supplier and top three in the world in terms of scale and technological advancement and created 863 research achievements and dozens of independent patents in four countries. Shanshan also gains investment returns through investment in Bank of Ningbo, Huishang Bank and other financial institutions and engages in financial leasing, commercial factoring and other financial businesses. The company successfully transformed from the first listed apparel enterprise to a leading enterprise in the new energy industry. Shanshan has becomes a diversified enterprise group with technology, fashion, financial services, urban complex and trade logistics as its major businesses.

Same Goal Achieved with Different Means

Diversification itself is not classified as good or bad, its management process is the key. The success of diversification lies in common resources and professional management. Common resources include management, capital, brand, technology, channels, etc. Youngor and Shanshan have established a good brand image throughout their early stage business with improved cash flow. This laid the foundation for the expansion of other businesses. Their good relationships with local governments also provide important support for the diversification.

For professional management, Youngor and Shanshan both apply the principle of "let professional people do their work". Hiring professional managers to manage industrial companies is an important method for enterprises to manage diversified businesses. In relation to authorization, two companies adopted different solutions. Shanshan appoints professional managers through the Board of Directors based on the headquarters" recommendation, and the headquarters fully delegates the operation to each industrial company, and manages companies through finance, internal control, audit, performance control, etc. Shanshan conducts an internal management analysis and evaluation and a performance audit twice a year. The performance appraisal of the management team focuses on the ROE, supplemented by growth and risk control indicators to fully encourage their creativity, initiative and motivation.

Youngor looked for professional managers from external resources. Meanwhile, Li Rucheng tightened his control over Youngor through equity control. By the end of 2020, Li Rucheng and his daughter held 98.73% of the shares of Ningbo Shengda Development Co. Ltd. to indirectly increase their holdings in Youngor. As a result they directly and indirectly hold 33.03% of Youngor.

Transformation Underwent by Hong Bang Tailors

For enterprises like Youngor, they do have a complete production chain, various sales channels in the domestic market and a strong brand influence; however, they went under tremendous pressure as inventories proliferated due to e-commerce consumption habits. The whole apparel industry has run into serious supply problems since 2013. Shanshan also faced the dilemma of high inventory levels, which added up to CNY 430 million, accounting for 48.7% of total assets in 2020.

Youngor and Shanshan are not alone in their journey to pursue diversification. Other leading apparel enterprises in Ningbo have also implemented diversification strategies: Taiping Bird entered into car sales, home furnishing products and commercial investment, and Romon ventured into real estate development and international trade. With increasing cash flow and inventory level brought by the development of apparel business, diversification is a must for enterprises in Ningbo when searching market opportunities and avoiding risks.

Besides the efforts taken by entrepreneurs, the huge demand of clothing as one of the basic necessities of our life is also an important guarantee for enterprises to handle external risks. "Two financial crises helped Youngor a lot and made us realize that our strength is still clothing", Li Rucheng said. Shanshan has successfully transformed into a high-tech enterprise. Zheng Yonggang once said to the media: "The era of making money by selling apparels has long passed. I prefer to be called a financier."

Questions:

【Case 7】

1. What is corporate-level strategy? Why is it important?

2. What are the drivers for apparel enterprises in Ningbo to pursue diversification?

3. Related diversification strategies or unrelated diversification strategy does Youngor and Shanshan adopt? Why?

4. Please evaluate the diversification strategies of Youngor and Shanshan.

Tips for answering the questions:

1. Corporate-level strategy is to solve the problem of how to gain competitive advantage when a company has multiple businesses. Apparel enterprises in Ningbo engaged in multiple businesses, it is important for the headquarters to consider how to allocate resources among business blocks.

2. This question can be answered in terms of the motivation for diversification. There are many reasons why a company adopts a diversification strategy, including finding a market with greater profit margin, avoiding risks, scope economy, industrial chain integration, and improving market influence.

3. Diversified strategy can be classified into different types depending on the levels of

diversification and interconnectedness among different businesses. According to whether multiple businesses can share resources, diversification is divided into related diversification and unrelated diversification.

4. The factors influencing the success of diversification strategy include: whether there is synergy between multiple businesses, whether there is excessive diversification, whether the increase of management difficulty is controllable, managers" diversification motivation, etc. Whether an enterprise should adopt diversification and what kind of diversification it should adopt requires weighing the benefits and risks that diversification may bring.

Case 8

The Integration of Enterprises in M&A: HISENSE's Acquisition of KELON

Key points:

the M&A strategy of a company, integration; influence factors in effective M&A;boycott of employees in M&A

Case Purpose:

This case introduces the process of HISENSE's acquisition of KELON, emphasizes the significance and value of integration in M&A, and guides students to understand the theoretical connotation of enterprise M&A strategy and the key factors affecting effective M&A.

Case Description:

After KELON was acquired by HISENSE, the company name was changed to HISENSE KELON Electrical Holdings Co., Ltd in 2007 (hereinafter referred to as "HISENSE KELON"). With the development of the company, in order to better reflect its actual main business and strategic positioning, meet the needs of brand management and brand development, the abbreviation of corporate A-share securities was changed to "HISENSE Home Appliance" in 2018. Thereupon, the full name of the company was changed from "HISENSE KELON Electrical Holdings Co., Ltd" to "HISENSE Home Appliance Group Co., Ltd". After years of development, HISENSE Home Appliance Group has become a super-large scale enterprise in the world focusing on home appliance manufacturing. Its main business covers R&D and manufacturing of refrigerators and other home appliances, domestic and abroad sales and after-sales service, and transportation of self-made products, etc. As of September 2021, HISENSE Home Appliance Group had a strong production capacity of an annual output of 13.5 million refrigerators, 18 million household air conditioners, 3.6 million central air conditioners, 3.4 million washing machines, 3.4 million freezers, over 1700 sets of molds (including over 900 sets of large plastic molds, over 200 sets of precision molds, over 600 sets of stamping molds), and over 200,000 tons of sheet-metal working, which were sold to more than 130 countries and regions. Therefore, viewed from the results of the acquisition, the "snake swallowing elephant" acquisition is very successful, but the process is not smooth.

Back in 2004, HISENSE Group had a variety of products, including color TV sets, air conditioners and refrigerators, with a total of sales volume of CNY 27.3 billion. At the same time, as a leading enterprise in white appliance industry, KELON Electrical had brands of refrigerators and air conditioners such as KELON, Ronshen, Combine and HuaBaoand had sales of CNY 8.4 billion. It was listed in A shares and H shares, controlled by Green Cool Group. Revealed by its Annual Report 2004, KELON's was No. 1 in the sales of refrigerator in China, with export increased by 87.5% and No. 4 in the sales of air conditioner in China. Therefore, if successfully acquiring KELON, HISENSE would become refrigerator leader and entered the first group of air conditioner in China. Merely viewed from the position of sales of refrigerator and air conditioner, the acquisition would certainly become a typical "snake swallowing elephant" M&A.

Originally, KELON was a township enterprise in Guangdong and started to produce refrigerators in 1984. It is one of the earliest refrigerator manufacturers in China. Ronshen refrigerator was also its sub-brand. By virtue of the label of pure China made refrigerator, high quality and brand awareness in early stage, KELON refrigerator was lionized by the market. However, KELON had become decayed due to unclear share ownership, internal corruptions and chaotic management. On April 29, 2005, a huge loss of CNY 60 million was reported in KELON annual report, and as of August 31, 2005, 108 litigation cases were related to it. Then HISENSE carried out field investigation and negotiations with local government. Finally Green Cool and HISENSE signed the transfer agreement on September 9, 2005 at transfer price being CNY 900 million.

However, due to continuous loss, financial institutions, suppliers and distributors lost confidence to KELON, and the company stopped production for a time. In the face of this situation, HISENSE intervened in the operation of KELON in advance to avoid the "blood losing" in the absence of finalizing the equity stake. HISENSE and KELON signed an exclusive sales agency agreement for the domestic market that HISENSE would buy KELON's products by injecting advance payment, and was responsible for providing goods to the merchants for cash returning, so as to assist KELON to promote products while preserve its sales system. At the same time, HISENSE sent more than 30 managers, including the General Manager, senior managers as well as middle level managers in financial, administration and marketing, to control the key positions and take over the management of KELON. They fully controlled KELON's cash flows as soon as they entered KELON.

While KELON restarted the production, KELON's organization adjustment plan was officially introduced, As a result, the number of departments at headquarter was reduced from 17 to 12, the number of management levels was reduced from 6 to 3. The power of General Manager of branch company was strengthened who was the chief of the organization. Domestic Marketing Company and Overseas Marketing Company were set up respectively, each had independent personnel and financial rights. The number of staffing was officially determined that redundant department and personnel were further cancelled. In contrast, before/after the takeover, there were 400/46 persons, 27/7 vehicles and 12/2 full-time secretaries in the headquarter.

The daily management of KELON was also adjusted. The starting afternoon working time of KELON was adjusted from 2:00 pm before the takeover to 1:30 pm. Accordingly, workers could go home half an hour earlier in the afternoon and the work efficiency was significantly improved. Through the implementation of attendance system such as clock in and clock out, the strict attendance system has changed KELON's previous practice that everything depended on the supervision of department leaders and the self-awareness of employees. After the takeover, KELON organized video training for the national sales system every month and held meetings with the sales managers of HISENSE to analyze the operation situation in last month and plan for the marketing of current month so that the business awareness of KELON's employees were strengthened. Employees who did not obey discipline would be criticized through circulated notice.

After the takeover, KELON's market share got a steady recovery. According to the statistics of China Market Monitor research institute, in November 2005, the market share of KELON's refrigerator products was 2.53 percentage points higher than that in July 2005, and the market share of air conditioner products was 1.62 percentage points higher than that in August 2005. Overseas sales in the fourth quarter of 2005 also achieved satisfied results. Refrigerator export in all three months of the fourth quarter increased by more than 97% compared with September. Air conditioner export in the three months in the fourth quarter were increased by 33%, 145% and 483% respectively compared with that of September. On April 21, 2006, KELON Electrical Appliance (000921) announced that its major shareholder, Guangdong GREENCOOL Enterprise Development Co., Ltd. had signed a supplementary share transfer agreement with Qingdao HISENSE Air Conditioner Co., Ltd. The former transferred its 26.43% share of KELON to the latter at a price of CNY 680 million. From then on, HISENSE began to implement comprehensive integration with KELON.

However, the cultural differences and collisions between HISENSE and KELON seem difficult to eliminate in a short time. The cultural integration launched by HISENSE was even seen as nit-picking. According to relevant information publicly disclosed, during over 20 years of KELON's history, important strategies, decisions, success or failure were all determined by the major shareholder and its representatives in KELON. The original executives of KELON had great resistance to the acquisition by HISENSE. They left one by one with the arrival of HISENSE's managers.

In February 2008, YANG Yunduo, HISENSE's "veteran", was appointed as Vice Chairman of HISENSE KELON Electrical Holdings Co., Ltd. With his efforts, the Board of HISENS passed the resolution to inject the assets of HISENSE refrigerator and air condition to KELON. On December 5, 2008, Zhou Xiaotian from Siemens was appointed as the fourth President of HISENSE KELON. Led by him, KELON achieved a smooth development. In 2009, HISENSE KELON's proposal to purchase the White Goods assets of its parent company Qingdao HISENSE Air Conditioner Co., Ltd by means of non-public issuance of A-shares was approved by China Securities Regulatory Commission, and the delivery of all assets was completed in the first quarter of year 2010. So far, HISENSE KELON has three "China Well-Known Trade Mark", namely HISENSE, KELON and RONSHEN, and also has four "China Famous Brand" products, namely HISENSE air conditioner, HISENSE refrigerator, KELON air conditioner, and RONSHEN refrigerator. The leading products cover many fields such as refrigerators, air conditioners, freezers and washing machines. HISENSE KELON's White Goods assets have been listed as a whole.

Up to 2021, a far-reaching change has been taken place in product types of HISENSE KELON, developing from a household appliance manufacturer producing refrigerators and household air conditioners to a comprehensive appliance manufacturer producing refrigerators, air conditioners, washing machines, kitchen appliances, environmental appliances, commercial cold chains, etc.

Questions:

1. The process of HISENSE's acquisition of and integration with KELON can be divided into two stages, please point them out.

2. What integration has been made in this case?

3. How does the employees' resistance in the target company affect M&A performance?

4. What are the key factors for an enterprise to effectively implement its M&A strategy?

Tips for Answering the Questions:

1. From KELON's crisis to HISENSE's takeover, until HISENSE KELON achieves its expected goal-using the listed company to integrate White Goods business, the process of HISENSE's acquisition of and integration with KELON can be divided into two stages. Students can analyze from the implementation process of the agreement.

2. The integration after enterprises M&A mainly includes business restructuring, financial restructuring and organizational restructuring. Business restructuring is to form new business combinations and new regional business distribution. Financial restructuring is to form new assets and financial structure. Organizational restructuring is to form a flexible and efficient organizational system. The three restructuring influence and cooperate with each other.

3. Employees' resistance will not appear immediately upon the integration, but will increase gradually with the deepening of the integration. At the initial stage of acquistion, Hisense sent its own senior executives to integrate Kelon, but the effect was not good. Until the appointment of Zhou Xiaotian, the fourth president, who moved from Siemens, the performance of M&A integration was improved.

4. The main factors hindering the success of M&A are: difficulties in integration, inadequate evaluation of M&A targets, huge or abnormal debts, difficulties in forming synergies, excessive diversification, managers' excessive attention to M&A, and excessive scale.

Case 9

Haitian: Sell Products to Places Throughout the World

Key points:

Analysis of internationalization motivation; identification of internationalization opportunities; internationalization entry modes and their suitable scenarios; knowledge of internationalization entry sequence; and relevant knowledge of internationalization of enterprises in emerging economies

Case Purpose:

Based on the international development of Haitian, a Niche Champion Demonstration Enterprise in the domestic injection molding machine industry, this case focuses on how Chinese injection molding machine enterprise entered the international market in fierce competition in the plastic machinery market, so as to understand how enterprises identify and make use of opportunities in the international market and how to solve difficulties, Finally, it helps students better understand the implementation and development of internationalization strategy.

Case Description:

China's injection molding machine has a history from the oldest manual injection molding machine to hydraulic manual, semi-automatic and full-automatic to today's all-electric injection molding machine, in which Haitian group played an important role. Today, Chinese market has formed an annual demand for injection molding machinery of about US $5 billion, and the supplies include home made equipment, imported equipment and JV equipment. The output value of domestic injection molding machinery has reached US $2 billion, of which Haitian Group has become No.1 in terms of annual output in China and even in the world.

In 1966, Jiangnan agricultural machinery factory, the predecessor of Haitian, was established. At that time, Haitian was just a small workshop producing sickles, hoes, water pumps and other agricultural machinery tools. Later, Zhang Jingzhang, founder of Haitian, saw that plastic shoes were not susceptible to worn, so he wondered how plastics were made. In 1972, Haitian's first injection molding machine came out, which opened the road of "attack" in the injection molding machine industry. In 1994, Haitian plastic machine production has ranked No.1 in the world in terms of output and has maintained its position so far. However, Haitian still has a clear understanding of itself and the industry. Zhang Jingzhang once said in the media, "We are No.1 in the world in terms of output but not technology." Through more active open learning and global R&D cooperation, Haitian was moving towards a broader space. Establishment of Haitian overseas subsidiaries was shown in Figure 9-1 in the chronological order. Haitian initially set up a subsidiary in Türkiye in 2001, taking the first step towards internationalization. Then in 2004, Haitian entered the Brazilian market and extended its overseas business to South America. In 2007, Haitian entered the European market for the first time, marked by the acquisition of Germany Zhafir, which was a milestone event of internationalization. Since 2010, Haitian

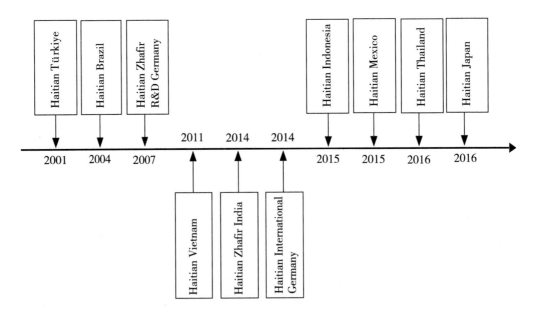

Figure 9-1 Haitian Internationalization Road

has entered Vietnam, India, Indonesia, Mexico, Thailand and other emerging markets, and established overseas subsidiaries; In 2016, Haitian entered the Japanese market and established a R&D center, achieving a qualitative leap in all electric technology.

1. Attempt in Türkiye

In 2001, Haitian Türkiye was set up, which was the first wholly-owned subsidiary overseas to provide sales and service support for local customers. Türkiye was located at the junction of Asia and Europe, with high cultural inclusiveness, and enterprises from Asia could integrate into it quickly. "As far as the final market of export products is concerned, it is found that some countries are copying China's development path, such as Türkiye." Zhang Jingzhang said that the needs of foreign customers were similar to those of domestic customers. Therefore, Haitian has always regarded Türkiye as an important export market and an important part of Haitian International's "globalization strategy".

Fu Nanhong, as the Technical Director, said, "the establishment of Haitian Türkiye has provided us with a new platform and will comprehensively improve our local sales and service level." The group planed to take Haitian Türkiye as the center, radiate the surrounding countries and regions, and fundamentally solve the problems of late delivery and difficult after-sales service of mechanical and electrical products in the world.

Due to the success in Türkiye, Haitian injection molding machine was recognized by the Ministry of Foreign Trade and Economic Cooperation as a "Famous Brand Export Commodity Highlighted with National Support and Development", and the export volume had increased year by year. In 2002, the company's export volume reached 35 million US dollars, won the "Overseas Market Development Award" by Ningbo government, and reached 50 million US dollars in 2003. The products were exported to more than 50 countries and regions including the United States, Europe, South America, Middle East and Southeast Asia. The output and sales volume ranked the first in China's plastic machinery industry.

In Haitian's internationalization strategy, the development of Turkish market was just an attempt, and Haitian had a larger strategic goal. However, in the west was strong European competitors with excellent core competence, and in the east was Asian customers with low consumption level. How could Haitian find a transition path?

2. Localization Strategy in Brazil

Haitian established a wholly-owned Brazilian subsidiary in 2004, mainly engaged in production, sales and service. It was expected that through the development in Brazil, the American market could be opened.

At that time, Haitian Brazil was lack of personnel in international business, nor did it has experience of overseas investment. With courage, Haitian Brazil completed the extremely difficult plan of founding and selling in the same year. Haitian Brazil insisted on localization and only sent three Chinese to Brazil to set up a Brazilian management team at the outset. Now, it seems that the wise strategy encountered many difficulties at that time, such as conflict of communication and culture. Haitian believed that clients couldn't be served better unless local system and culture was well learned. From selling products to selling services, taking the road of service-oriented manufacturing is the only way for enterprises to enter the high-end link of the industrial chain.

3. Learned from Germany

From 2001 to 2007, Haitian was preparing for entering the high-end international market. In the end of 2005, Haitian hired Professor Franz, the President of the German Plastics Machinery Association to act as member of the Haitian Development Strategy Committee. After Haitian's acquisition of Zhafir in 2007, Professor Franz officially joined Haitian Group and served as the Executive Vice President of the Group. He was responsible for coordinating Ningbo R&D department and Germany Zhafir R&D center to jointly develop all-electric injection molding machines. Through the joint efforts, technical breakthrough for HTD was made and the machine performance had been greatly improved. In October 2007, Haitian successfully developed Zhafir Tianrui VE series injection molding machines.

In 2014, Haitian Germany was successfully established. Cooperation with German companies could dated back to 1995 when Franz, Director of Norman Snow Group, visited Haitian. Three years later, the two parties jointly established Demag Haitian Plastic Machinery Co., Ltd., specializing in high-end injection molding machines. The German processing technology and management concept had a far-reaching impact on Haitian's future development.

After initially entering the international market, Haitian was faced with the problems of technical barriers and production needs. Haitian Germany accelerated technological change on one hand and considered orderly expansion in the international market on the other hand. "The best way to keep up with your competitors is to face your competitors directly. Only by going deep into Germany can you develop rapidly," said Xiang Linfa, General Manager of Haitian International Germany. He preliminarily decided that Haitian would go to Germany to establish a company. Shi Huajun, Head of the Internal Control Department and General Manager of the Investment Relations Department of Haitian Group, said that "at that time, many domestic plastic products were expensive because their equipment depended on imports. The large machine market was monopolized by foreign countries, so we had the determination and goal to enter the equipment manufacturing." In addition, feeling the competitive pressure and the need for growth, improving service capacity and strengthening pre-sales and after-sales service, etc. were all important factor for Haitian Group to consider when making decisions on investment in German plants.

After Germany, Haitian has successively established wholly-owned subsidiaries in India, Indonesia, Mexico and Thailand to go deep into the markets of South Asia, North America and Southeast Asia in the form of wholly-owned factories and invest in the markets of emerging economies on a large scale.

4. Expanding in India Market

The successful establishment of the company in India is mainly due to the development environment of the plastic industry in India. About 37% of the injection molding machines sold in India in 2008 were imported, much higher than 11% in 2002. More than half of the imported machines came from China. Since 2009, the Indian government and competent authorities or relevant institutions had helped develop the local injection molding machine industry. In 2014, Haitian had ranked first in production and sales in the world.

The downstream industry of India's injection molding machine industry was developing vigorously. They also welcomed machines from China. The new plant buildings established by the Indian Customs had finished machine inventory, spare parts inventory, mold test center and training center, provided more sufficient area, expanded production capacity, shortened delivery cycle, and efficient and convenient service and support to local customers. It has greatly improved the satisfaction of the Indian government and market.

5. Plant Building in Mexico

On May 28, 2019, Haitian Mexico held a groundbreaking ceremony for its new factory in Guadalajara, Mexico's second largest city. It's set up was to realize the localized production and assembly of Haitian injection molding machine products and meet the needs of the Mexican market and was one of Haitian's export platforms. Zhang Jianming, the Executive Director and President of Haitian, said that the construction of the new factory was one of the important strategic layouts of Haitian to promote its global business. In the future, Haitian would comprehensively improve its production efficiency on the basis of the new factory, and continue to create value for customers with better products and more convenient services through technological innovation, service innovation and management innovation. This new factory is also the first injection molding machine manufacturing base in Mexico. Mexico, as the second largest plastic consumer market in Latin America, has huge market demand and broad development prospects. Since 1999, Haitian has started the sales and service of injection molding machines in the Mexican market. As of 2018, Haitian's annual sales in the Mexican market accounted for 40% of China's total export of injection molding machines. Haitian has become one of the most trusted brands in the plastic processing industry in Mexico.

6. R&D Base Established in Japan

The improvement of technology was credited with successful opening of overseas subsidiaries. From hydraulic injection molding machine to all-electric injection molding machine, Haitian had always made great efforts in technology development in order to catch up with the pace of international advanced technology. In 2016, Haitian Japan was established to carry out technology R&D and product sales services. This action was a big jump for Haitian to catch up with the world-class plastic machine technology. Learning the technology of all-electric energy-saving models in Japan was critical to Haitian's development in the world.

The strategy of Haitian Japan was different from that of Haitian subsidiaries in other countries, not only in the profit growth point, but also in the lateral industry development. Due to the increasingly fierce competition in the domestic plastic machinery industry, the establishment of R&D centers in Japan aimed to both learning technology and entering the Japanese market, so as to protect the domestic market. "Haitian Huayuan Japan Machinery Co., Ltd." established in Japan on April 1, 2016 had further improved the sales and service level of Haitian in Japan, providing perfect pre-sales and after-sales services for local customers. Haitian International's development in the Japanese market would play a linkage effect and strive to achieve a new breakthrough in the global strategic layout.

Haitian also actively cooperated with local enterprises. Niigata Machinery Technology and Haitian Group had established a joint venture in Japan. The JV would focus on the development of electric injection molding machine technology and enable Niigata to use the large-scale production technology of Haitian to produce high-precision Japanese molding machines in Japan at a lower cost. The whole chain of Haitian needed to rely on industrial cooperation, so the quality shall be improved. Haitian chose to start with electroplating Haitian learned the Japanese model and began to build its own electroplating workshop. Haitian was still making continuous R&D investment, benchmarking and launching competition against Engel of Austria, who was No.1 in the technology of large-scale injection molding machine, and marching towards the goal of overall leading in the technical level.

Through reviewing the process of international footprint of Haitian, it is not difficult to find that its entry into the international market began with overseas sales and adopted the agency system. After several years of efforts, Haitian products have basically gained a firm foothold in the overseas market, but only in the medium and low-end market before the year of 2007. After acquiring Zhafir in 2007, Haitian had accelerated its overseas market expansion, established branches, factories and technology centers in Japan, etc. Developed countries had become the main target markets for exports.

Haitian has built a perfect product portfolio and realized the full coverage of the plastic processing industry chain. Under the background of recovery of domestic market and improved layout of the overseas business, Haitian launched the third generation of injection molding machines in 2018. The rapid product iteration further consolidated the Haitian's leading position.

Then, Haitian made efforts in the high-end market in 2020 and implemented the strategy of "full electrification of small tonnage injection molding machines and two-platen large tonnage injection molding machines". The development of Zhafir electric series was more robust. It is expected that it will achieve a compound growth rate of more than 30% in the next three years. As of 2020, Haitian had established subsidiaries in 9 overseas countries, had its own agents in more than 60 countries and sold products to 130 countries around the world, and the road of internationalization is getting farther and farther. In 2021, Haitian's sales of injection molding machines increased by 35.7% to a record CNY 16 billion, with more than 56,000 machines delivered. Its sales in China increased by 33% year on year, while its overseas sales reached CNY 4.93 billion, with a year-on-year growth of 40.1%. Its export volume exceeded 10,000 units for the first time. Haitian's market share in North America, Southeast Asia, Europe and South America increased. The annual sales of

Haitian's main product series Mars rose steadily by 33.2% to US $1.7 billion.

Haitian plans to radiate the surrounding countries and regions of the four global centers (China, Türkiye, Brazil, Germany) and challenge the high-end market on par with European injection molding machines.

Questions:

【Case 9】

1. What are the main reasons for Haitian to enter the international market?

2. What internationalization strategies did Haitian mainly adopt?

3. According to the route of Haitian to open subsidiaries overseas, analyze the order in which Haitian entered other countries, and what is the reason for this order? What are the rules?.

4. How should Haitian deploy its future globalization strategy?

Tips for Answering the Questions:

1. This question is about the motivation of enterprise internationalization, which can be considered from the perspective of international competition, disadvantages of source countries, and dynamic capabilities. Based on the theory of internationalization motivation, opportunity recognition and internationalization of emerging economies, this case analyzes how China's injection molding machines enter the international market in today's fiercely competitive plastic machinery market.

2. Internationalization strategy mainly includes globalization strategy, multinational strategy and transnational strategy.

3. This question can be answered through analyzing the difficulties and opportunities faced

by Haitian in the development process from the perspective of internationalization motivation, internationalization opportunity identification, etc., to show the entry mode used by Haitian in different situations. Due to the blockade of core technologies, high service costs and the scarcity of professional maintenance personnel in China, Haitian has been blocked from accelerating its development. It hopes to go out and build its brand better, so it started founding of overseas subsidiaries and opened the first one in Türkiye. After years of overseas business experience, Haitian opened a subsidiary in Germany, which is a breakthrough in the European market and a turning point in Haitian's internationalization process.

4. In combination with the internal and external environment of the enterprise, you can put forward suggestions on Haitian's future market selection and strategy formulation for internationalization.

Case 10

The Cooperative Strategies of JD.com

Key points:

Strategic Alliances; Business-level Strategic Alliances; Corporate-level Strategic Alliances; International Strategic Alliances

Case Purpose:

Through the introduction of the cooperation strategies of JD.com, this case guides students to understand the meaning and categories of strategic alliances, identify the strategic alliances at corporate-level, strategic alliances at business-level and international strategic alliances, and think about the differences and connections of different types of strategic alliances.

Case Description:

At the beginning of 2014, JD.com entered the final stage of preparation for listing on NASDAQ. After the large-scale products category expansion in 2012 and the complete change of corporate logo in 2013, JD.com had built itself into a large-scale comprehensive e-commerce platform, with the proportion of third-party sellers constantly increasing. However, in the face of Taobao and T-Mall, JD.com is under great operating pressure. Under the circumstance that its main business continued to suffer losses and sales and administrative expenses soar, how to further expand viewership data imports, increase commodity trading volume and improve profit margin had become the core issue that JD.com executives always pay attention to.

1. JD.com's corporate-level cooperation with Tencent

JD.com, who was eager for network traffic portal, had found common ground in cooperation with Tencent, the Internet giant. For JD.com, it urgently needed the introduction of huge amount of traffic brought by social media. While Tencent had two mobile portals, Wechat and QQ, with a huge user base, strong stickiness and huge viewership data. As for Tencent, although it had successively invested in Yixun, Buy.qq.com and Paipai.com, these e-commerce companies didn't work well in developing offline logistics and warehousing business, while JD.com had accumulated abundant experience in logistics and warehousing construction. If the partnership could be realized, JD.com would be able to get product information through Wechat and QQ's advertising push. Tencent could transfer its weak e-commerce business to JD.com to focus on games and media business that Tencent was good at, and also support JD.com to become a powerful counterforce to Alibaba who was trying to enter the social software market. For Tencent, such cooperation is profitable in the short term and of strategic value in the long term. For JD.com, joining hands with Tencent enabled JD.com to gain a significant competitive advantage far beyond Amazon, Ebay and Dangdang, making JD.com possible to compete with predominant Taobao and T-Mall.

In March 2014, JD.com and Tencent announced the establishment of a strategic alliance, in which JD.com transferred 15% of its shares to Tencent in exchange for Level 1 entry to Wechat and Mobile QQ Apps. At the same time, it acquired all the equity, personnel and assets of Tencent's online shopping website Buy.qq.com and Paipai.com as well as minority equity of Yixun.com. In May 2014, when JD.com listed on NASDAQ in the US, Tencent increased its stake by 5% as promised. Following the deal, JD.com met a soaring in mobile orders in the fourth quarter of 2014, which had increased 372% and the proportion of mobile orders had also reached 36% of all JD.com orders.

In October 2015, JD.com and Tencent announced the launch of the strategic cooperation project "JD-Tencent Plan", in which the two parties would build an innovative marketing platform named brand-commerce by combining the massive user data of each other. The plan is to provide brand merchants with accurate portraits, multidimensional scenes, quality experience of the full range of marketing solutions. On the one hand, the data of JD.com could provide information about user characteristics, behavioral preferences, advertising preferences and buying preferences. On the other hand, the data of Tencent could provide information about demographic characteristics, life style, interests and hobbies, and usage environment. As Tencent's social data had connected with JD.com's transaction data, it is possible to understand customers' characteristics in a deep level and accomplish targeted advertising, thus effectively realizing precise marketing.

At the end of July 2016, Tencent and JD.com jointly launched the marketing platform "JD-Tencent Cube". The main idea of JD-Tencent Cube was to find user characteristics with specific consumption habits through big data, and find specific groups that meet the characteristics and push targeted and accurate advertisements to them. In this way, users would be able to receive information about the products they like or need, and manufacturers would be able to accurately deliver their products to potential customers. During the 2016 Double Eleven Shopping Festival, with the help of JD-Tencent Cube, many well-known brands on JD.com platform doubled their user scale and sales volume. JD.com and Tencent also got a lot of advertising revenue through the marketing services provided by JD-Tencent Cube.

With the progress on big data technology, in the updated marketing solution "JD-Tencent Cube Plus", launched in April 2018, JD.com and Tencent could integrate users' data to analyze and predict users' brand preferences. The JD-Tencent Cube Plus could further realize refined brand marketing and more accurately tap potential customers with high purchase propensity for specific brands, raising the level of digital marketing to a higher level. The key to the success of the cooperation of JD.com and Tencent is the alignment of their strategic visions and goals. After Tencent integrated the social platform, content platform with JD.com transaction platform, it was possible to realize the intelligent connection between online and offline scenarios in the retail industry, which not only improved consumers' consumption experience, but also provided effective marketing means for merchants. The significance of the deep cooperation of JD.com and Tencent went far beyond the value of mere network data imports.

2. JD.com's business-level cooperation with Internet companies

While cooperating with Tencent to reshape China's e-commerce landscape, JD.com had also made strategic alliances with other Internet companies. In September 2016, JD.com announced a comprehensive strategic alliance with Bytedance Technology, to launch the "JD-Toutiao Plan" which mainly covers three aspects. First, JD.com opened a Level 1 shopping entrance "JD-sale" on Toutiao App, with the help of JD.com e-commerce open platform JD-Kepler, consumers could enjoy e-commerce shopping services in Toutiao App without the need to log in JD.com; Second, JD.com implemented precise advertising based on Toutiao's big data capabilities; Third, the two parties jointly carried out e-commerce cooperation based on interest-based reading, and helped more content creators on Toutiao to realize traffic data monetizing through shopping guide and commission sharing. Toutiao's 550 million user base had laid the foundation for the success of the JD-Toutiao Plan.

In August 2017, JD.com and search engine giant Baidu jointly launched a strategic alliance framework called the JD-Baidu Plan which also covers three aspects. First, JD.com would open a Level 1 shopping entrance "JD-sale" on Baidu's App, which would also be directly connected to JD.com's e-commerce open platform JD-Kepler. Second, Baidu would deeply cooperate with JD.com's e-commerce data with the data pool generated by its massive product matrix and user base to help JD.com, the brand partners and merchants on JD.com platform to realize precise advertising. Third, the two parties would carry out cooperation through the mode of guide purchase and commission sharing to improve traffic data monetizing of content creator. With the support of Baidu's leading AI technology, JD-Baidu Plan was leading in accuracy and response speed of precise advertising.

By duplicating the well-established "JD-X" model, JD.com had established strategic alliances with Qihu360, Netease, Sogou, Iqiyi, Sohu and Sina by April 2018. In terms of business relationships, the nine Internet companies – Tencent, Bytedance, Baidu, Qihu360, Netease, Sogou, Iqiyi, Sohu and Sina – are media to JD.com. By cooperating those largest traffic entry portals in each segment, JD.com is able to cover almost 100% of Chinese

Internet users and user scenarios. In this case, brands registered in JD.com only need to purchase relevant marketing services within the system so that it automatically achieved comprehensive and precise advertising to consumers on various Internet ports. Meanwhile, no matter what kind of interface consumers used to purchase goods, they would eventually be directed to the JD.com page of merchants and achieve one-stop delivery with the help of JD.com's efficient logistics system. In this way, the cooperation of JD.com with Internet enterprises enabled merchants and customers to be directly connected without being restricted by channels and scenarios, thus realizing "borderless retail".

3. JD.com's cooperation with offline companies and international companies

As well as cooperating with online Internet companies, JD.com was also building partnerships with offline companies.

In August 2015, JD.com announced a 10 percent stake in Yonghui Superstores for CNY 4.31 billion. JD.com's investment in Yonghui Superstores aimed to strengthen JD.com's biggest advantage – the self-operate sale-logistic system, namely procurement, warehousing, distribution and after-sales. Both parties agreed to strengthen alliance coordination, regularly carried out high-level communication and discussed major cooperation issues, actively explored online and offline cooperation mode and online-to-offline (O2O) business development, form cooperation in warehousing and logistics, and jointly explored Internet financial resources. After becoming a shareholder of Yonghui Superstores, the JD-to-Home Services and Yonghui Superstores could realize complementary advantages and enhance their competitiveness.

In June 2016, JD.com announced an in-depth strategic alliance with the international retail giant Walmart, in that JD.com would acquire all the equity and assets of Walmart's online store "YHD.com" through the newly issued and transferred JD.com common shares with a market value of $1.5 billion to Walmart. Through cooperation with Walmart, JD.com could strengthen its business layout in the O2O field through Walmart's resource advantages in retail, and realize globalization strategy with the help of Walmart's overseas resources and price advantage of supply chain and supermarket products. In addition, as YHD.com was influential in the east China market, this acquisition would make up for JD.com's market weakness in this region and bring much-needed supermarket category resources to JD.com, thus effectively warding off the attack of T-Mall and Suning.

In June 2017, JD.com announced a $397 million investment in Farfetch, a British luxury e-commerce company, to enter the luxury market. JD.com believed that Farfetch's unique luxury channel would be able to attract many Chinese customers. JD.com would not interfere in Farfetch's independent operation, but would provide support for Farfetch's business in China in terms of marketing, logistics, payment and other technologies.

In December 2017, JD.com and Tencent signed a strategic alliance agreement with VIP.com, in that JD.com and Tencent purchased 5.5% and 7% of VIP.com's equity respectively. Under the agreement, VIP.com would have access to Wechat wallet and JD.com platform. Since VIP.com's dominant business is focused on women's clothing, beauty makeup and maternal and child products, while JD.com's biggest advantage is digital appliances, the combination of the two would realize the complementarity of users and product categories. Since then, JD.com had further carried out in-depth cooperation with VIP.com in overseas warehouse and supply chain. VIP.com would open 12 overseas warehouse resources to JD.com to provide high-quality overseas warehousing and logistics services for JD.com's global purchasing business, while JD.com would open nearly a thousand overseas transportation route to VIP.com.

In June 2018, Google announced a $550 million investment in JD.com, noting that the two companies would work together to develop retail solutions in multiple regions of the world and explore the infrastructure for the next generation of retail, including unmanned stores, unmanned shelves, and intelligent logistics equipment. As a test of the partnership, JD.com had selected a set of high-quality products to sell in several regions of the world through e-commerce company owned by Google. The partnership with Google would put JD.com in a better position to expand globally. JD.com hoped to enter the European market in 2019 to compete with Amazon.com, and the partnership with Google would help make that happen.

4. Epilogue

By cooperation with other enterprises, JD.com had been able to gain a foothold in the highly competitive e-commerce market. While consolidating its own logistics system as the core competitive advantage, JD.com made up for its own shortcomings to achieve complementary advantages and realize multi-win. In 2019, JD.com's net revenue reached nearly CNY 580 billion, up nearly 25% year on year, and its gross merchandise volume exceeded CNY 2 trillion for the first time. In 2021, JD's annual revenue hit a record CNY 951.5 billion, surpassing Alibaba's revenue of CNY 234.3 billion. It could be concluded that, growing with the tough competition with Alibaba, JD.com had found a proven successful development path through cooperation.

Questions:

1. Based on the case, recall the modes of strategic alliance, and link the different cooperation strategies of JD.com with different modes of strategic alliance.

2. Based on the case, analyze which strategic alliances of JD.com belong to the business level strategic alliances and what their objectives are.

3. Based on the case, analyze which strategic alliances of JD.com belong to corporate level strategic alliances and what their objectives are.

4. Based on the case, analyze which strategic alliances of JD.com belong to international strategic alliances and what their objectives are.

Tips for Answering the Questions:

1. There are three main ways to realize strategic alliances: joint venture, equity strategic

alliance and non-equity strategic alliances. Readers can judge the mode of strategic alliance based on the equity arrangement of the strategic alliance and the situation of the alliance companies described in the text.

2. Business-level strategic alliances are cooperation strategies used to enhance core competitiveness in a given business domain, and help enterprises achieve success in a single business area. Business-level strategic alliances mainly include complementary alliances, competitive response alliances, and uncertainty reduction alliances. Since explicit and implicit collusion can reduce competition intensity and social welfare, it violates market principles and is generally not referred to as a strategic alliance. Readers can find business-level strategic alliances among those cooperation that only enhance competitiveness in a given business domain.

3. The corporate-level strategic alliances are cooperation strategies adopted to expand the business scope or enhance cross-business core competitiveness. Among them, diversification strategic alliances refer to strategic alliances that achieve diversification by sharing resources; synergistic strategic alliances refer to strategic alliances that create economies of scope and achieve synergistic effects by sharing resources; franchising refers to a cooperation mode in which the franchisor authorizes the franchisee to use its trademark or business model and receives franchise fees and commission fees. Readers can find corporate-level strategic alliances with the criteria whether a cooperation strategy achieves diversification, creates synergistic effects, or cooperates through brand and trademark authorization.

4. International strategic alliances are strategic alliances that share resources with foreign companies to create competitive advantages. Readers can judge whether an alliance is an international strategic alliance by whether the cooperation crosses national boundaries.

Case 11

Corporate Governance Evolution of Vanke

Key points:

ownership centralization; compensation incentives for the management; Board of Directors; market for corporate control, defense tactics.

Case Purpose:

By introducing the corporate governance characteristics of Vanke and several events related to corporate governance it undergone, this case intends to guide the students to understand the impact of decentralized ownership structure on the development of Vanke featured by professional manager system, and help them understand the advantages and disadvantages of different types of incentive compensation programs, and the interactivity and complexity between attack and defense in the market for control power.

Case Description:

Vanke, namely China Vanke Co., Ltd. was founded in 1984, entered the real estate market in 1988, and was listed in Shenzhen Stock Exchange in 1991 as the second listed company of Shenzhen Stock Exchange. As a pioneer and leader in the real estate market of China, Vanke experienced a lot in its development process. But it maintained a steady growth by keeping up with the times. Vanke has ever been listed in Forbes "Asia's Fab 50" and won the rewards of best corporate governance and best investor relations recognized by international authoritative media for many times. It is the "most appreciated Chinese company" published by "Fortune (Chinese version)". In the "Research Report on China's Top 100 Real Estate Enterprises" issued by the Enterprise Research Institute of the Development Research Center of the State Council, Institute of Real Estate Studies, Tsinghua University, and China Index Academy, Vanke was always ranked among the top three most powerful China's real estate enterprises over years and it won the championship of the most powerful Chinese real estate enterprises from 2006 to 2016.

As a private joint-stock enterprise managed by the founder management team based on the professional manager system, Vanke established sound and modern management systems and standard and transparent governance structure which were widely recognized by all walks of life for a long time. However, as a representative enterprise, Vanke has also experienced a series of representative corporate governance events which were all closely related to Vanke's unique equity structure. Unlike most Chinese listed companies of which the ownership structure is highly centralized, Vanke's ownership structure is relatively decentralized. From 1991 to 1999, the largest shareholder of Vanke was the state-owned Shenzhen New Generation Industry Co., Ltd. (abbreviation as the New Generation) and its parent company Shenzhen Special Economic Zone Development Co., Ltd which held 6%-9% shares of Vanke as the only shareholder with more than 5% shares. From 2000 to 2015, the largest shareholder of Vanke was China Resources Co., Ltd. (abbreviation as China Resources) whose shareholding ratio was maintained at about 12%-15%. Considering the great influence of Vanke's management team in the industry, especially the founders Wang Shi and Yu Liang, all of the substantial shareholders including New Generation, Shenzhen Special Development Zone Co., Ltd. and China Resources gave support and tacit consent to the decision-making power of the management team of Vanke. The corporate governance of Vanke, which was dominated by the founding management team as tacitly permitted by the substantial shareholders and featured by decentralized ownership structure, helped Vanke avoid the malady brought by "one dominant shareholder" and "insider control" that occurred to most Chinese enterprises. But it also led to a lot of new issues and challenges to Vanke.

1. The threatening but not dangerous battle between Jun'an and Vanke
As a threatening but not dangerous episode, the "battle between Jun'an and Vanke" occurred in 1994 became the first event that a decentralized ownership structure caused risks in the corporate control of Vanke. In 1993, the stock price of Vanke fell because it did

not achieve the expected performance target. Some minority shareholders were dissatisfied with the operation of Vanke. On March 30, 1994, Jun'an Securities, Vanke's underwriter, held a press conference on behalf of the four shareholders including the New Generation (6.5%), Hainan Securities (1.1%), Dragon Hill (HK) Investment Co., Ltd. (1.7%) and Chuangyi Investment Co., Ltd. (1.5%) and issued a "Proposal for Reform" jointly with them, which pointed out the problems with the management team of Vanke and suggested reorganization of Vanke's business structure and management team. After the conference, the Chairman, Wang Shi, immediately contacted the leaders of New Generation and persuaded them to withdraw from the alliance with Jun'an and make a statement. In the morning on March 31, 1994 Vanke announced suspension so that Jun'an was unable to manipulate the stock market. On April 1, 1994 the founder Yu Liang went to Hainan by plane and got the support of Hainan Securities. On April 2, 1994 Vanke issued an announcement stating that the management of Vanke has obtained support from the New Generation and Hainan Securities and the management still kept stable and robust control over the company. In the morning of April 4, 1994 Vanke's stock trading was resumed and rose to the limit-up, and in the afternoon of that day, Vanke held a press conference, announcing that the "battle between Jun'an and Vanke" ended.

The "battle between Jun'an and Vanke" did not impact the actual control of Vanke's management over the company. Since then, Vanke achieved rapid development. But good performance was also accompanied by new problems because the management team of Vanke does not own significant shares of the company. The number of middle and senior managers kept increasing but they could not share the strategic benefits from the rapid development of the company because they do not have ownership on the company shares. They lack the sense of belonging. The shareholders of Vanke also worried that such situation may lead to shortsighted behavior of the management and they need incentive measures to motivate the management team. In such cases, how to further design the ownership structure and motivate the efforts and creativity of the management team through incentive compensation design became the new corporate governance issues faced by Vanke for realizing long-term development.

2. Vanke's three incentive compensation programs

From 2006 to 2014, Vanke took three incentive compensation programs.

From 2006 to 2008, Vanke implemented its first incentive compensation program in the way of restricted shares. The first incentive compensation program was open to all middle and senior managers and key business members. A special incentive fund was established and a third party was engaged to purchase A shares of Vanke in the secondary market, and grant such shares as incentives to the employees who met the performance conditions. Vanke set two conditions for the incentive: (1) performance: the annual fully diluted return on net assets should exceed 12% in that year; (2) stock price: the annual earnings per share in the year should increase by more than 10% and the stock price should increase year after year. However, only in 2006 the conditions were met and the shares were granted. In 2007, the condition for stock price was not satisfied because of the tailspin of Chinese stock market. In 2008, the conditions for performance were not satisfied because as affected by the sub-loan crisis in the United States, China adopted tightening monetary policies and the volume of real estate transactions decreased significantly. Obviously, the first incentive compensation program did not achieve the desired results because the conditions for incentives contained external factors beyond the control of employees.

After the first incentive compensation program failed, many key employees felt frustrated and the morale of the company was low. Moreover, a new round of regulation of the real estate industry began since 2010. The real estate industry faced much uncertainty. In order to attract and retain the key employees, Vanke implemented the second incentive compensation program from 2011 to 2013. The second incentive compensation adopted the stock option method, under which employees qualified may buy a certain number of shares of the company within a certain period of time in the future under the predetermined conditions. This incentive program was applicable to 838 middle and senior management members and the key business employees. A total of 110 million stock options were established to encourage the employees who meet the exercise conditions to purchase the shares of Vanke at a low price and then sell them at the market price to make profit. By drawing lessons from the first incentive compensation program, the second program only put requirements on performance indicators, that is, the annual fully diluted return on net assets in 2011, 2012, and 2013 should exceed 14%, 14.5%, and 15% respectively.

Compared with the first incentive compensation program, the second one was exercised successfully because its indicators were more reasonable. But it brought by more serious problems. As the stock price of Vanke was significantly undervalued and in a long time the market price was even lower than the option exercise price, the incentive was less attractive. Furthermore, the employees had to purchase the incentive shares with their own money. The high cost required for exercising the option further reduced the possibility of option exercise. In addition, under the management of the successor Yu Liang, the business focus of Vanke moved from residential buildings to commercial buildings. As a result, a number of executives resigned. According to statistics, a total of 4 (out of 8) Executive Vice-Presidents and 3 (out of 7) Vice-Presidents left Vanke during the period from 2011 to 2014. Accumulatively, the employees who left accounted for 36% of the persons qualified for stock option incentive. After leaving Vanke, these people, who did not obtain the incentives as expected, selected to join other real estate companies, start their own businesses, or turn to the popular Internet companies.

Yu Liang made self-examination on the failure of the two incentive compensation programs. He realized that a good incentive compensation program should be able to stimulate the subjective initiative, enthusiasm and creativity of the management team and enable the professional managers to share the achievements and risks of the company. After one year, Yu Liang worked out the business partner mechanism and released the third incentive compensation program in May 2014. Finally, 1320 middle and high-level managers and general employees were identified as the first batch of business partners. The business partner mechanism of Vanke consists of three parts: (1) granting shares to the business partners: each of the business partners signs an trust agreement under which a third party fund management firm, Ying An Partnership Fund, was engaged to manage all of his/her share in the company profit, bonus, and collective bonus account. With this income, Ying An Partnership Fund is authorized to purchase A-shares of Vanke in the secondary market and make investment through financing leverage. At that time, the shares of Vanke managed by Ying An reached about 4% of the total shares. (2) Co-investment program: for a new project to be invested by Vanke, the direct management personnel of the project should also make investment while other employees may participate in the investment voluntarily. (3) Event Partner Management: For a particular event, Vanke may set up a special partner group to deal with the event. Not limited by the traditional scope of work of functions and responsibilities, the group may coordinate with different departments to find the best solution and after the event is resolved, the event partners return to their original departments and positions. In this way, the project management level of Vanke became flat, creating a coordination mechanism among various departments.

The business partner mechanism significantly stimulated the enthusiasm of the middle and high-level managers of Vanke. Since 2014, the financial performance of Vanke continued to improve and its stock price rose steadily. The key to the success of the business partner mechanism lied in the delegation of power and the change of status of the managers. Under such a mechanism, the employees qualified for the incentive gained more authorization and became the managers and risk-takers of a certain business. Their linkage with the resulting interests and risks helped give full play to their initiative.

3. The rumbling battle between Baoneng and Vanke

Just at the moment that the business partnership mechanism made a success and the development of Vanke was improving, Vanke encountered the biggest crisis since its establishment – the battle for control power with Baoneng. In 2015, the government of China launched measures to stimulate the depressed real estate industry suffering from oversupply. At the same time, since the stock market in China was in a downturn, the stock price of Vanke dropped significantly. It drew the attention of Yao Zhenhua, the leader of Shenzhen Baoneng Corporation which focused on financial, comprehensive property development, and modern logistics businesses and conducted capital operation through Foresea Life Insurance and Shen Zhen JUSHENGHUA Co., Ltd. Yao Zhenhua considered that if Baoneng could acquire substantial shares of Vanke to take control over it, its scale of commercial real estate development would be multiplied and could also raise huge capital by replying upon the reputation of Vanke to achieve tremendous growth. Even Baoneng could not obtain the control power over Vanke, it could sell the undervalued shares at high prices. It is definitely profitable.

On July 10, 2015, Foresea Life Insurance of Baoneng purchased 553 million shares of Vanke. But it did not attract Vanke's attention. Later within 160 days, Baoneng purchased another 2681 million shares of Vanke by high leverage financing through various channels. Thus, Baoneng acquired a shareholding ratio of 24.26% and became the largest shareholder of Vanke in place of China Resources (15.29%). Baoneng's significant increase of its shareholding ratio in Vanke in just five months with tens of billion CNY caught Vanke's management off guard and shocked the market. Wang Shi has ever objected to the acquisition intention of Baoneng because Wang Shi thought that Vanke was the model of mixed-ownership enterprises of China, for which the largest shareholder should be a state-owned enterprise and Baoneng was not qualified for a major shareholder of Vanke. This reflected the views of Vanke's management. Baoneng has ever carried out radical measures to replace the management team of CSG Holding after acquiring it. So the management team of Vanke believed that once Baoneng took control over Vanke, it would be highly possible to dismiss lots of members of Vanke management. Vast investors also thought that if Baoneng controlled Vanke, it would certainly overturn the stable and dedicated operation strategy of Vanke and destroy the status and corporate reputation.

On December 18, 2015, in order to prevent further increase of Baoneng's shareholding ratio in Vanke, the management team of Vanke applied for suspension of Vanke's A shares on the grounds of proposed "major asset reorganization", and held an emergency meeting to discuss the countermeasures. They wished to find a "white knight" to expel Baoneng. Wang Shi made requests to China Resources for increasing its shares in Vanke for several times, but it was refused by Fu Yuning, Chairman of China Resources. On January 15, 2016, Vanke issued an announcement which claimed that during the suspension period, Vanke had entered into an intent of cooperation with the potential counterparty and it applied for further suspension to complete further verification. On March 12, 2016, Vanke issued a public announcement indicating that it entered into a memorandum of cooperation with Shenzhen Metro Group Ltd. (Shenzhen Metro), a large wholly state-owned enterprise in Shenzhen under which the two parties would conduct major asset reorganization at a consideration of CNY 40-60 billion in the way that Vanke issued new shares to Shenzhen Metro. At first, Baoneng and China Resources accepted this reorganization transaction. But later they suddenly disagreed. On the evening of June 23, 2016, Baoneng made a statement expressing its objection to the investment of Metro to Vanke and stated that it would vote against such transaction at the general meeting in August. Unusually, China Resources also made a statement on its official WeChat account in support of Baoneng. China Resources stated that it objected to the reorganization transaction proposed by Vanke's management and it only accepted business cooperation of Vanke with Shenzhen Metro, and furthermore, it challenged the compliance and validity of the Board of Directors of Vanke in the process of deliberating and voting on the reorganization transaction.

At this critical moment, one of the independent directors of Vanke, Hua Sheng made public his objection to China Resources and Baoneng. Hua Sheng deemed that: (1) Vanke's achievements today were inseparable from the sound modern enterprise management system it formed under the long-term acquiescence of China Resources. But for Baoneng's offer of acquisition of Vanke shares, China Resources did not communicate with Vanke's management, but instead, it began to interfere with the enterprise management framework abnormally to damage the management ecology of Vanke. He believed that it was undesirable. (2) China Resources objected to the reorganization on the grounds that some assets in the intent of cooperation were not valued reasonably. It was very shortsighted and improvident. (3) As compared to Shenzhen Metro which could bring high-quality assets to Vanke, Baoneng's real estate businesses, far behind Vanke in all aspects, could not make contribution to Vanke's development, but would bring a series of problems such as horizontal competition and conflict of interest. (4) Although China Resources was opposed to the reorganization transaction, it did not propose any alternative. If, as interfered with by China Resources, the reorganization transaction between Vanke and Shenzhen Metro failed and the stock price of Vanke dropped, China Resources would not be able to protect the interest of small and medium investors.

On June 26, 2016, Baoneng made an application to the BOD of Vanke for holding an interim general meeting and proposing removal of 10 directors and 2 supervisors, including the Chairman Wang Shi and the CEO Yu Liang. The BOD had no choice but to delay. On July 4, 2016, just as Vanke resumed trading in A-share market, Baoneng acquired shares of Vanke further and increased its shareholding ratio to 25%. According to the Articles of Association of Vanke, a controller whose shareholding ratio reaches 30% would directly become the controlling shareholder of Vanke.

At such a critical juncture, the largest natural person shareholder of Vanke sent a public letter of accusation to the China Securities Regulatory Commission (CSRC) and other six regulatory ministries and commissions to strongly condemn Baoneng and China Resources and request protection of the rights and interest of small and medium investors. He claimed that Baoneng and China Resources should disclose the interest relationships and secret agreements between them, explain the reason for flip-flopping on the reorganization transaction with Shenzhen Metro, and called on the two to make a statement that they were not engaged in any insider trading and market manipulation. He pointed out that Baoneng was suspected of using illegal funds and non-compliant intermediary to purchase and control listed company.

On July 22, 2016, the CSRC intervened in the "battle between Baoneng and Vanke" and interviewed the heads of Baoneng and Vanke. It criticized their acts which seriously affected the market image and normal production and operation of them and violated their obligations of corporate governance, and required them to safeguard the interest of small and medium shareholders, stabilize the order of capital market, and restore normal operation. On t December 5, 2016 the CIRC issued an announcement to suspend the new universal insurance related business of Foresea Life Insurance. Since August 4, the long-time rival and also friend of Vanke, China Evergrande started to acquire the shares of Vanke until its shareholding ratio reached 14.07%. But China Evergrande was not intended control Vanke and its investment in Vanke was presented as financial assets for sale in the accounts. On January 12, 2017, China Resources announced that Shenzhen Metro would acquire all shares held by China Resources and its subsidiaries in Vanke. On Jan. 20, 2017 the acquisition agreement was approved and Shenzhen Metro acquired 15.31% shares of Vanke and China Resources withdrew with considerable earnings. Since then, China Evergrande announced on March 16 of the same year that it would cooperate strategically with Shenzhen Metro by delegating 14.07% of its voting rights to Shenzhen Metro for a term of one year. Since then, in the equity structure of Vanke, the total shareholding ratio of the supporters of the current management team and management system of Vanke, namely Shenzhen Metro (15.31%) and China Evergrande (14.07%, who granted its voting rights to Shenzhen Metro), Vanke's management, Vanke Ying An Partnership Fund (7.12%) and the largest natural shareholder (1.21%), reached 37.71%, surpassed that of Baoneng (25.4%), and maintained the control power over Vanke.

On February 24, 2017, the CIRC imposed a removal and disqualification for insurance industry penalty for 10-year on Yao Zhenhua, then Chairman of Baoneng's Foresea Life Insurance on the basis of serious violation of laws and regulations found in the inspection on Baoneng's Foresea Life Insurance.

On 30 June, 2017 Yu Liang was successfully elected as the new Chairman of Vanke, and thus Vanke's management team and enterprise management systems were maintained.

Later, Baoneng gradually transferred the shares it held in Vanke and the battle between Vanke and Baoneng ended.

4. Epilogue

It is shown from many years' development process of Vanke that the decentralized ownership structure and the professional manager model helped Vanke establish unique governance model and advanced management systems, but also brought a series of challenges and crises. Nowadays based on the experiences in the situations in the past, Vanke's equity structure has become more centralized and the business partner mechanism has also achieved remarkable results. We may look forward to the further steady development of Vanke in the real estate industry under the new situation featuring strict regulation.

Questions:

1. Based on the case, what is the impact of Vanke's decentralized ownership structure on Vanke's governance?

【Case 11】

2. Based on the case, describe the advantages and disadvantages of different types of compensation incentive programs? Discuss why the business partner program made a success?

3. Based on the case, discuss the important role of the Board of Directors in corporate governance, and the identity and role of independent directors?

4. Based on the case, describe what defense strategies did Vanke take in the battle with Baoneng.

Tips for answering the questions:

1. Decentralized ownership and centralized ownership are both double-edged swords.

For decentralized ownership, the major problem lies in the shareholder's lack of control over the management, leading to the primary principal-agent problem between the shareholder and the management, manifested as the conflict between the board of directors and the management (especially the CEO). As for centralized ownership, the major problem is the dominance of majority shareholders over the company, leading to the primary principal-agent problem between majority shareholders and minority shareholders, which is manifested as the conflict between independent directors and dependent directors and management. In addition, enterprises with highly centralized ownership are generally capable to resist hostile takeovers from external markets. However, enterprises with decentralized ownership may face higher risk of external market acquisition.

2. Whether the compensation incentive program is effective involves many factors, as whether the exercise conditions are reasonable, whether the exercise cost is appropriate, whether the incentive program includes the sharing of decision-making rights and other non-economic incentive measures. Therefore, the effectiveness of incentive compensation program often depends on the match between the program and the scenarios, and a perfect compensation incentive program should consider all possible situations and put forward corresponding solutions.

3. The board of directors plays different roles in different scenarios. When the operation of the firm is sound, the board of directors does not play a significant role in the routine management activities. However, when serious corporate governance events occur, the board of directors would become the main battlefield for the control of the company. In this process, the competition for directors' seats directly determines the interests and voice power of shareholders. According to relevant Chinese laws and regulations, independent directors are positioned as independent forces independent of majority shareholders, and can play the role of arbitrator when there are conflicts between majority shareholders or between majority shareholders and minority shareholders, thus having crucial impacts on the results of interest conflicts within the company. In many domestic listed companies,

independent directors do not often oppose majority shareholders by "objection" or "veto", but are more likely to passively protest majority shareholders by "abstention", "absence" or "resignation".

4. There are various defense strategies. The commonly seen defense strategies include "poison pill" (after a hostile takeover, the original shareholders are eligible to buy new shares or bonds at a discount, thus diluting the acquirer's equity), "golden parachute" (after a hostile takeover, buyer must pay the target company's top management members huge relocation compensation), "delay" (manipulating the agenda of board of director to suspend or delay a shareholder meeting), "white knight" (asking friendly companies to takeover the focus companies and expelling malicious buyers), "litigation" (by suing the acquirer, intervene its attention and delay the purchase behavior). These strategies can hinder and delay the acquisition behavior of buyers.

Case 12

The Organization-Structural Evolution of Xiaomi

Key points:

The Evolution Pattern of Enterprise Strategy and Structure; Matching between Business-Level Strategy and Functional Structure; Matching between Corporate-Level Strategy and Business Unit Structure

Case Purpose:

By introducing the evolution of strategy and structure of Xiaomi since its foundation, this case guides students to understand the co-evolution of corporate strategy and structure, identify the matching between different types of functional structures with different business-level strategies, the matching between different types of Business Unit structures with different corporate-level strategies, and think about the design principles of organizational structure.

Case Description:

On April 6, 2010, in the Yingu Building near the Baofusi Bridge in Beijing, Xiaomi was founded by the former CEO of Kingsoft and angel investor Lei Jun, and six cofounders

1. A booming start-up

As a start-up, Xiaomi's shares were held by all employees. the co-founders plus early stage employees, there were merely 56 members in the company, including President Lei Jun and Vice President Lin Bin (former vice president of Google China Engineering Research Institute), Zhou Guangping (former senior director of Motorola Research Center) who led the mobile phone production team, Liu De (former Dean of Industrial Design Department of University of Science and Technology Beijing) who led the mobile phone industry design team, Li Wanqiang (former head of Kingsoft Iciba) who led Xiaomi.com and e-commerce team, Hong Feng (former senior product manager of Google China) who led the MIUI system development team, and KK Wong (formerly engineering development director of Microsoft Chinese Academy) who led the MiTalk team. Mobile phone, e-commerce, MIUI and MiTalk were Xiaomi's four core businesses in its start-up stage.

In order to reduce market risks, Xiaomi did not directly enter the mobile phone industry at the outset. Instead, based on the in-depth optimization of the Android system, Lei Jun took the lead in launching the operating system MIUI and social software MiTalk, attracting a large number of enthusiastic users "Mifans" to participate in the improvement and polishing of MIUI system through MIUI online community, Weibo and other ways. With a detailed understanding of users' needs, Xiaomi laid the groundwork for designing and building its first smart phone. In October 2011, Xiaomi officially released the dual-core 1.5 Ghz smart phone Mi 1, priced at CNY 1,999, and limited to online sales only. The first 300,000 phones sold out in five minutes. That tremendous demand helped Lei Jun see the bright future of China's smart phone market, and prompted Xiaomi's meteoric rise.

In 2012, Xiaomi integrated the industrial design with the production of mobile phones and set up the mobile phone department. Meanwhile, Xiaomi.com turned to be the e-commerce department. The MIUI system and Mitalk also set up independent departments. In order to maintain creativity, Xiaomi adopted a flat organizational structure in its early stage, the top layer is Xiaomi's five co-founders, and the second layer is the middle-level managers who are the cornerstones of Xiaomi's business, and the third layer is the frontline employees. Since frontline employees could interact directly with users, this helped Xiaomi fully explore and meet users' needs in the R&D process. At the same time, for different R&D projects, project team was set up and any engineer could apply to become a project manager. In addition to leading the development and daily management of the team, the project manager is also responsible for coordinating and communicating with other departments.

With the help of the flat organizational structure, Xiaomi's employees could devote themselves to product development, gave full play to their subjective initiative, and kept consistent with the company's strategic goals while flexibly and quickly responding to customer needs. In this way, Xiaomi had been able to form a benign working atmosphere and created innovative products that met consumer needs.

On August 12, 2013, Xiaomi launched Redmi phone online, with 7.45 million users taking pre-orders and 100,000 units sold out within 90 seconds. During the Double-Eleven Shopping Festival in 2013, Xiaomi online store became the first store whose revenue exceeded CNY 100 million and got the most sales of mobile phone in a single store, while the Xiaomi brand received the most attention on smart phone market. On the back of its impressive performance, Xiaomi raised a new round of funding in 2013 with a market valuation of 10 billion dollars.

2. The temporary pain of diversification and internationalization

Since 2013, Lei Jun began the diversification of hardware. Internally, Xiaomi began to laid out hardware at the network traffic entry end, focusing on developing Mi TV, Mi box and Mi router. To this end, Xiaomi set up a new Mi box and TV department, toned down further development of MiTalk and set up a router and cloud services department. Externally, Xiaomi laid out the intelligent hardware field through venture capital and built an "ecological chain plan". This plan aimed to expand Xiaomi's product line, tried to cut into hundreds of segments through the duplication of Xiaomi model, drove the development of the entire intelligent hardware industry. Since then, Xiaomi had set up an Ecological Chain BU, which then launched Xiaomi earphones, power banks, wristbands, blood pressure monitors, air purifiers and smart furniture sets. By the end of 2016, Xiaomi had invested in 77 smart hardware eco-chain companies, of which 30 had released products, 16 had annual revenue of over CNY 100 million, 3 had annual revenue of over CNY 1 billion, and 4 had an estimated value of over 1 billion dollars, and those companies had accumulated more than 7,000 patents in total. While developing ecological chain hardware, Xiaomi and Kingsoft also invested 230 million dollars in 21Vianet.com at the end of 2014 to arrange cloud services and big data business in advance. Therefore, Xiaomi's original strategy of "mobile phone, TV, router" had been upgraded to a new strategy of "mobile phone, TV, router + ecological chain".

In order to adapt to the diversified businesses, Xiaomi employed a mixed mode of BU organization structure and network organization structure. Besides functional departments such as legal, internal management, public relations and financial investment departments, a large number of business unit such as Electronic Commerce, Routers and Cloud Service, MIUI, Mi box and Mi TV departments employed the BU organizational structure, while the Mi Ecologic Chain BU and Mutual Entertainment BU adopted the network structure as an incubation matrix, where Xiaomi company is at the core, connecting a series of relatively independent ecological chain enterprises.

At the same time, Xiaomi also made steady progress in internationalization. Xiaomi brought in Hugo Barra, the global vice president of Google Android, to promote this process. Then, Xiaomi quickly entered into markets in Singapore, Malaysia, Philippines, India, Brazil and Indonesia by signing contracted phone sales agreements with local operators and combining online promotion with offline sales. After building on success in emerging markets, Xiaomi had made inroads into Europe and the US and started to enter Africa with lower-end phones.

However, while Xiaomi was focusing on ecological chain and diversification, its core business — mobile phones — had encountered serious problems. Since Mi phones were initially sold with high-cost performance, its technology reserve was weak, which made its pattern easy to be imitated. After the success of Xiaomi's pattern, some domestic brands such as Meizu, OnePlus, Honour etc. had imitated this pattern to launch a series of cost-effective mobile phones, which quickly occupied the market through online and offline channels. At the same time, Xiaomi's failure to keep up with the supply of core components such as chips and screens had hampered the launch of new phones and subsequent shipments. In 2015, its growth rate was only 6.18%, and its market share fell to the fourth place. In 2016, its shipments declined and its market share fell out of the top five. Not only that, Xiaomi's reputation was also affected by negative news, such as patent ban in India.

In the face of adversity, Lei Jun took charge of the mobile phone supply chain from May 2016 and rearranged the head of the mobile phone department. Since then, Xiaomi had revitalized its phone product line with the launch of milestone high-end full-screen phone Xiaomi MIX and large-screen phone Xiaomi Note4. At the mobilization meeting of Xiaomi Mobile phone department on July 7, 2016 Lei Jun encouraged the employees to start from scratch again. Since then, Lei Jun had tried to grant the Xiaomi brand the identity of high performance and fashion, while Redmi brand were set to carry the identity of cost-effective performance.

While overcoming the crisis, Xiaomi had reorganized its organizational structure. As its business scope and complexity continued rising, business chain continued extending, Xiaomi also suffered from complex organizational redundancy, excessive management scope and difficulties in coordination and management. As a result, Xiaomi started to simplify and implement hierarchy reforms which refined the functions of employees, promoted the specialization of BU and reduced the scope of management while most R&D, technological, internal management, product and decision-making departments still maintained a flat organizational structure.

3. New sail

On July 9, 2018, with the successful listing in Hong Kong, Xiaomi launched a new iron triangle strategy as "extensive hardware + new retail + Internet services". In terms of extensive hardware, the new strategy highlighted the role of smart phones and core hardware products as Xiaomi's network traffic entrance. In terms of new retail, it highlighted the comprehensive expansion of ecological chain products with the help of offline channels of Xiaomi Store and online channels of Mi.com. In terms of Internet services, it focused on the development of MIUI, advertising business, Xiaomi Youpin and financial services to obtain value-added services. Xiaomi had also established a diversified policy with cloud computing as the core and ecological chain as the main axis.

To carry out Xiaomi's new strategy, Lei Jun changed the organizational structure of Xiaomi. On July 31, 2018, Xiaomi adjusted the organizational structure of the Ecologic Chain BU. As the business of the Ecologic Chain BU was further enriched and the personnel were further increased, the previously flat structure had encountered numerous coordination and management difficulty. After this adjustment, the Ecologic Chain BU was further stratified, Investment Department, Exploration Products Department and Precious Metals Department were newly set up, the previous Supply Chain team, Business Analysis team, Quality Control and Architecture team was further divided into departments with higher specialization.

On September 13, 2018, Xiaomi made its largest organizational restructuring since IPO. The basic principle of this restructuring was to separate decision-making department, organization department from other functional departments, expand horizontally the business units. During this adjustment, part of the R&D team of previous MIUI BU was incorporated into Phone BU, the other departments were split and combined into new business units, namely Big Home Appliance, (new) Ecosystem Chain, Notebook Computer, Intelligent Hardware, Xiaomi IoT Platform, Product E-commerce, and Internet business units (responsible for different types of software development and content business). The new 10 business units indicated a shift in Xiaomi's business focus. In terms of functional departments, in addition to maintaining the Financial Department and Industrial Park Department, the previous Marketing Department (except the public relations team), the E-commerce Team and the New Media Team of the Sales & Service Department were integrated into the (new) Sale, Service & Marketing Department, and the Public Relations Team in the former Marketing Department was upgraded to the Public Relations Department. The most important restructuring was the establishment of the Organization Department and the Staff Department. Xiaomi was able to centralize the decision-making and personnel rights, which were originally dispersed in various BUs, so as to ensure a unified and orderly implementation of the strategy. As a result, Xiaomi maintained its original advantages of flat management while carrying out hierarchy reform.

In December 2018, to improve the unsatisfactory sales of Xiaomi phones in China, Lei Jun carried out a comprehensive reorganization of the Sales, Service and Marketing Department which was split into two parts. The domestic sales teams were consolidated into China Division, while the foreign sales teams (except for the Indian market where Xiaomi was set up separately) were consolidated into the International Division. The newly adjusted China Division highlighted the great importance attached to the Chinese market, especially strengthening the development of the domestic offline market and improving the sales of high-end smart phones. In June 2019, in order to further strengthen the sales management of Xiaomi mobile phones in China, Lei Jun personally assumed the position of the President of China Division and carried out a hierarchy reform.

4. New strategy and in-depth change

Lei Jun had made in-depth structural adjustments to the Mobile Phone BU and the AI BU, in order to implement Xiaomi's "mobile phone + AIoT" plan as to implement the pan-hardware dual-engine policy of the new Iron Triangle Strategy.

On February 18, 2019, Lei Jun announced that he was about to adjust the said BU to improve Xiaomi's R&D and innovative capabilities and enhance the stability of the component supply chain. In this adjustment, the Design Department and the Quality Department remained unchanged, the original Mobile Phone Cost Department was updated to the Staff Department which was fully responsible for operation, business and cost accounting. The previous Mobile Phone Core Device Department was transformed into the Hardware R&D Department, and the R&D investment in audio devices was increased. Meanwhile, the Display Touch Control Department was newly created, which aimed to develop under-screen-fingerprint technology. The brands of Xiaomi mobile phones were also adjusted to five major brands: Xiaomi, focusing on the middle and high-end market; Redmi, focusing on the youth and overseas market; POCOPHONE, focusing on the Indian market; Meitu, licensed by Meitu focusing on the female mobile phone market; and Black Shark, invested by Xiaomi, focusing on the professional game mobile phone market.

On February 26, 2019, in order to enhance the strategic significance of AIoT, AI and cloud technology, Xiaomi created the Group Technical Committee, and subsequently created the AIoT Strategic Committee, which was used to coordinate the direction and standards of AI and IoT technology application in the development of various Xiaomi products. Meanwhile, Xiaomi separated the original AI and cloud platform team into Artificial Intelligence BU, responsible for the AI technology and Xiao AI product; Big Data BU, responsible for the large data, search and recommend business, and Cloud Platform BU, responsible for cloud technology development and the operation and maintenance of cloud platform. In addition, Xiaomi had further set up Internet BU 5 which was responsible for overseas application development, and the Internet Commercialization BU which was responsible for domestic Internet commercialization planning. Xiaomi had already made deployment on the development of IoT: In terms of application software, IoT cloud platform and Mijia App had been opened to promote the development and utilization of application software; in terms of computing, Kingsoft Cloud had been developed; in terms of communication network, Mi box and Mi Router had been developed to effectively connect various terminals; and lastly, in terms of interactive devices, Xiaomi had invested in more than 200 small ecological chain enterprises over the past few years, and as many as 150 million IoT devices were connected to the network in 2018.

Subsequently, Xiaomi set up the Group Quality Office, and in July 2019, Xiaomi set up the Group Procurement Committee and the Group Design Committee. So far, Xiaomi had reorganized its functional structure and established six core functional departments at the group level, namely Group Finance Department, Group Staff Department, Group Organization Department, Group Quality Committee, Group Procurement Committee and Group Technical Committee. Since then, Xiaomi had still adjusted the company's organizational framework, but the basic structure for research and development, sales and functional organizational structure had been stabilized.

5. Epilogue

By the end of 2019, Xiaomi had evolved from a start-up with 5 project groups and 56 members in 2010 to a huge multinational enterprise group with 28 functional departments and BUs and over 17,000 full-time employees. Appropriate organizational structure and effective strategy complemented each other, promoting another performance rising of Xiaomi. Data show that in the second quarter of 2021, Xiaomi's global market business continued to break through, with market revenue reaching a record high of CNY 43.6 billion, up 81.6% year-on-year. Xiaomi ranked second in the world, with a market share of 16.7%, and ranked first in 22 countries and regions.

Questions:

1. Based on the case, what is the general pattern of the collaborative evolution of corporate strategy and structure? How it is reflected in the development of Xiaomi?

2. Based on the case, what are the advantages and disadvantages of flat structure and hierarchy structure? Why Xiaomi employed flat structure as a start-up venture? Why Xiaomi employed a mixed structure consisted of flat structure and hierarchy structure when it grew larger? Why didn't Xiaomi employ hierarchy structure completely?

3. Based on the case, what is the logic of Xiaomi's restructuring of its organizational structure? Why some were modified to BUs while the others remained conventional?

4. Based on the case, why did Xiaomi's business structure adjustment accelerate significantly after its listing in 2018? Will the restructuring of Xiaomi gradually stop or continue in the future?

Tips for answering questions:

1. The collaborative evolution pattern of the corporate strategy and structure is general along this order: First, the Simple Structure (applicable to focus strategy); Second, the Functional Structure (the flat structure applicable to differentiation strategy, the hierarchi-

cal structure applicable to cost leadership strategy, and the hybrid structure applicable to the integrated cost leadership/differentiation strategy); Third, the Business Unit Structure (the competitive mode applicable to unrelated diversification, the cooperative mode applicable to correlated constrained diversification, while the strategic business unit mode applicable to correlated linked diversification). Readers can compare this sequence with the development history of Xiaomi.

2. The flat structure had the advantages of good responsiveness and strong tolerance for innovation, which is suitable for R&D and decision-making departments. The advantages of the hierarchical structure are clear division of labor, high professionalism and high unity of management, which is suitable for business units whose tasks are easy to split but scale is large.

3. Business reorganization is generally initiated to solve the problem that different business units are unable to create synergistic effect and that the management and coordination cost of those businesses is too high. In order to carry out business restructuring, the organizational structure needs to match with it. The advantage of division structure is that it provides space and opportunity for independent development and decision-making, and can calculate income and profit independently, so its performance can be measured by financial performance. However, as it is difficult for some departments to independently calculate their income and profit, these departments can only be assessed by means of strategic performance, instead of adopting the division structure to carry out simple financial evaluation.

4. The structure of the corporate must match up with its environment and corporate strategy. When the environment is complex and protean, the enterprise's structure will frequently change. If the businesses face less uncertainty, the structure of the related departments will also be stable.

Case 13

Ren Jianxin, the Founder of ChemChina

Key points:

Strategic leadership; strategic leader; key strategic leadership action; managerial succession

Case Purpose:

By introducing the story of entrepreneur Ren Jianxin who founded and developed ChemChina, this case guides students to analyze and understand the nature of strategic leadership, identify key strategic leadership actions, and consider the possible impact of managerial succession on enterprises.

Case Description:

A "BLUESTAR" Rising from the Northwest

In 1984, Ren Jianxin, the Secretary of Communist Youth League of the Chemical Machinery Research Institute (CMRI) of the Ministry of Chemical Industry in northwestern city Lanzhou discovered an abnormal set of statistics: boiler limescale in China consumes more than 8.5 million tons raw coal each year, and the essential cause is the poor industrial cleaning technology in China. While seeing this fact, it occurred to Ren that the technology called "LAN-5" could solve the problem of boiler limescale theoretically. "Lan-5", with its full name "nitric acid industrial corrosion inhibitor", is a corrosion inhibitor technology developed by the CMRI for 5 years, and has won the third prize of national technical invention. However, the invention was left unattended in the archives for a long time. At that time, there were no industrial cleaning enterprises in China, and all projects involving industrial cleaning were undertaken by foreign companies. Facing the opportunity of domestic industry cleaning market, Ren decided to borrow CNY 10,000 from the CMRI with his property as collateral and was allowed to establish a cleaning company in a form of "collective contracting". The BLUESTAR cleaning company was founded in the institute's air-raid shelter.

As the "LAN-5" technology could thoroughly clean the coal boiler scale and greatly improve the service life of the boiler, BLUESTAR created a revenue of CNY 320,000 in the first year of business.

In view of BLUESTAR's lower price, excellent effect, the business of BLUESTAR developed rapidly, and "LAN-5" technology was also implemented in many industries. After 1988, BLUESTAR undertook the pre-operation cleaning business of large complete sets of petroleum, petrochemical, chemical, non-ferrous metallurgy and electric power equipment introduced from abroad during the period of the Seventh Five-Year Plan to the Tenth Five-Year Plan. In a few years, BLUESTAR rapidly expanded and grew into a professional cleaning corporation with the most complete categories of cleaning technology and the strongest ability on comprehensive cleaning in China.

As the industrial cleaning business was at high-speed income growth and in short supply, Ren believed that China was about to embrace a large-scale industrialization process, and there was an urgent need for a mature industrial cleaning industry, and BLUESTAR alone could not meet the national demand. Therefore, Ren chose to promote industrial cleaning technology nationwide. By 1994, there were thousands of enterprises mastering cleaning technology, creating nearly 30,000 employees in the cleaning industry and nearly CNY 10 billion benefits for the country.

BLUESTAR Progressing in Adversity

In 1996, BLUESTAR was listed in A-share panel in China. In order to provide the company a wider development space, Ren applied to to move BLUESTAR's headquarters to Beijing. At the end of 1996, Mrs. Gu Xiulian, the then-minister of Ministry of Chemical Industry, inaugurated BLUESTAR's new headquarter. After moving to Beijing, BLUE-

STAR had gained broader development space and opportunities. After the industrial cleaning market became matured, BLUESTAR determined to seek new business growth points through mergers and acquisitions. At the same time, there are some large and old state-owned chemical enterprises in predicament, if BLUESTAR can merger and acquire and restructure these state-owned resources, the company would be able to rapidly expand its scale and business. As a result, Ren took the initiative to serve as the leader of the reform and management team of the Ministry of Chemical Industry, and promoted BLUESTAR to start a series of mergers and acquisitions of old chemical SOEs in China since 1996.

The first target of merger is the Spark Chemical Plant, a SOE whose major product is organic silicon. Although organic silicon is an indispensable high-tech material for the development of cutting-edge science and technology, China could not make scale production. In order to break the foreign monopoly of organic silicon production, Spark Chemical Plant introduced 10,000-ton organic silicon device which had been tested 28 times within 5 years. All the tests failed resulting in a huge loss of CNY 140 million. The debt ratio of the Spark Chemical Plant was as high as 200%, and more than 10,000 employees and their family members have no income and many of them had quitted their jobs to make a living.

Seeing this chemical plant on the verge of bankruptcy, Ren Jianxin determined to implement critical reform from administration and techniques. In order to understand the real situation of the plant, Ren had direct contact with the front-line workers through various means. In the face of historical problems, Ren implemented the first ever policy that all staff were laid off and had to compete to get re-recruitment, therefore reducing staff and increasing efficiency. In order to realize the successful operation of the production line, Ren collected and brought back a large number of technical documents from abroad, recalled a large number of technical staff who left their posts, and invited experts in China and abroad to discuss and modify the transformation plan. After 5 months of hard work, in the 29th test run succeeded, making China the fifth country capable of large-scale production of organic silicon.

Since the merger with the Spark Chemical Plant, BLUESTAR started its new business on new materials industry. In the following years, after four rounds of large-scale mergers and reorganizations, BLUESTAR successively acquired dozens of state-owned chemical enterprises including Nantong Synthetic Materials Factory, Chenguang Chemical Research Institute, etc. While leading a number of SOEs to get out of difficulties, BLUESTAR has become the leader of the new chemical materials industry, and its assets had exceeded CNY 20 billion, in which the production value of bisphenol A and special epoxy resin ranks first in China, the production value of organic silicon ranks first in China and the third in the world.

After acquiring a large number of chemical enterprises, in order to integrate and optimize its business structure, BLUESTAR once laid off 40% of all employees. However, Ren made great efforts to create new employment opportunities for laid-off employees. By founding Malan Ramen and Zhongche Auto Repair, BLUESTAR provided many jobs for laid-off employees and their families.

ChemChina Going Global

In 2002, BLUESTAR was upgraded to be one of the large and medium-scale SOEs directly administrated by State Assets Supervision and Administration Commission. Faced with the incoming fierce international competition after China's entry into WTO, Ren proposed to the State Economic and Trade Commission a construction plan of China's "big chemical industry" to comprehensively improve the competitiveness of Chinese chemical industry. This plan aimed to construct a large enterprise group as large as PetroChina and Sinopec by further acquiring and integrating chemical enterprises spreading around China. In 2004, the China BLUESTAR (Group) Corporation and China HaoHua Chemical (Group) Corporation merged to establish China National Chemical Corporation (ChemChina), in which Ren Jianxin served as the CEO. After the establishment of ChemChina, Ren put forward the strategic positioning of "Old Chemical, New Material", the core of which is neither upstream competition for resources, nor downstream competition for market, and strive to achieve win-win or multi-win situation, leading a path of value creation for the harmonious development of the industry.

In order to further enhance ChemChina's technological competitiveness, Ren launched a new round of upgrading activities from a indigenous company to a global one, with overseas acquisitions as the main means. Based on the international vision that BLUESTAR developed in the 1990s when it set up joint ventures abroad and the M&A capability that BLUESTAR developed in domestic market, ChemChina began to aim overseas mergers and acquisitions. To ensure the success, ChemChina hired world-class professional service agencies and experts and introduced Blackstone Group, the largest private equity firm in the US as a strategic investor. After full preparation, Ren set the target of M&A as the leading enterprises in the global chemical sector. Since 2006, ChemChina has acquired nine leading enterprises in France, Britain and Germany, which has achieved remarkable synergies and good performance. Among them, as one of the world's three largest nutritional additive companies acquired in 2006, the France Adisseo's sales revenue increased by 4 times and profit increased by 22 times, and it was successfully listed in China. ADAMA, an Israeli pesticide company acquired in 2011, saw its profit increase by more than two times in 2016, becoming the sixth largest pesticide company in the world. Ren believed that the success of oversea M&A of ChemChina mainly depended on cultural integration, and the key to realize cultural integration was respect and learning. By 2017, Ren has completed what was by far the largest overseas acquisition in China's history, the $43 billion purchase of Syngenta, which ranked second only to Monsanto and DuPont in agricultural chemicals. By taking this opportunity, ChemChina has successfully entered the first echelon of global agricultural chemical industry and laid a solid foundation for China's food security in the field of seeds and pesticides.

After the completion of a series of overseas acquisitions, ChemChina's business layout as "material science, life science, advanced manufacturing technology and basic chemical", as known as the "3 + 1" business structure, became more and more clear, and with the process of operation and management of these world-class chemical enterprises overseas, the domestic companies has absorbed lots of valuable knowledge and experience, which greatly improved the technical level and management ability of ChemChina.

The New Journey of Sionchem Holdings

Ren Jianxin announced his retirement as Chairman of ChemChina in June 2018. The successor is Ning Gaoning. Although they are both M&A experts, Ning's leadership style is different from Ren's. Compared with Ren's gentle strategy of maintaining highly independent operation of overseas M&A enterprises, Ning paid more attention to the implementation of large-scale and in-depth integration in overseas M&As. In May 2021, ChemChina and Sinochem announced the reorganization and merger to establish a giant enterprise "Sinochem Holdings", in which Ning Gaoning continued to serve as the Chairman.

As the largest consumer and producer of chemicals in the world, compared with developed countries, China still has many issues such as low degree of refinement, low level of science and technology, low rate of informatization and comprehensive integration, and relies heavily on imports for high-end chemical products. After the establishment of an essential comprehensive large multinational chemical enterprise, Sinochem Holdings will challenge international chemical giants such as BASF, Bayer and Dow DuPont to change this situation,

Questions:

【Case 13】 1. Based on the case, what is the strategic leadership? Why strategic leadership is so important to firms?

2. Based on the case, what are the key strategic leadership actions reflected in Ren's leadership behavior?

3. Based on the case, what changes will be made by an external leader with a markedly different management style from his predecessor.

Tips for Answering the Questions:

1. Strategic leadership is the ability to anticipate events, look ahead, preserve flexibility, and motivate others to make needed strategic changes.

2. Key strategic leadership actions generally consist of five aspects: setting strategic direction, effectively managing the company's resource portfolio, maintaining an effective organizational culture, emphasizing ethical principles and establishing balanced organizational control.

3. An external management successor usually brings about significant strategic change.

Case 14

Strategic Entrepreneurship of Bosideng-A Domestic Brand in Down Garment Industry

Key points:

entrepreneurial opportunities; internal entrepreneurship; strategic entrepreneurship; invention; innovation; imitation

Case Purpose:

Through the analysis on Bosideng's internal entrepreneurship practices, this case intends to guide the students to understand entrepreneurial opportunities and think about the process of strategic entrepreneurship.

Case Description:

On November 27, 2019, a co-branded down garments jointly launched by Bosideng Jean Paul Gaultier attracted widespread attention of fashion stars and celebrities and heated discussion of the fashion media.

Bosideng was established in 1976. In 1992, the founder Gao Dekang boldly introduced advanced production lines and created the "Bosideng" brand. Since 1995, Bosideng has maintained its No. 1 position in terms of sales in the down garment industry in China for 15 consecutive years. In 2007, Bosideng was listed in the Hong Kong Stock Exchange, the first company in the down garment industry of China, achieving its leap from a "Chinese brand" to a "world brand". But since 2010, it encountered the biggest difficulties since its establishment.

1. Bosideng in Crisis

At the outset, Bosideng encountered great pressure from domestic and international competition. In China, the brands such as Semir, Youngor, and Septwolves made a big push into the down garment market and gradually occupied the down garment market by relying on their advantages in style, pattern, color design and mainstream channels. Several sports brands such as Lining and Anta also launched sports down garment series. In the international market, the brands such as Uniqlo also entered the down garment industry, and even the luxury brands such as Armani also accelerated their expansion in the down garment market in the Asia-Pacific region.

Secondly, Bosideng faced tremendous changes in the market demand. It was ageing rapidly as an old brand. In the eyes of consumers, Bosideng was a brand designed for "middle-aged and elderly women" due to its dull style, backward marketing model and poor performance in development of new products. In addition, the operation of Bosideng also had many problems. The offline stores were heavily overstocked while expanding rapidly, Bosideng Group could not obtain the latest market information in a timely manner, and its product category and layout were not reasonable enough to meet the needs of consumers. As a result, the capital chain of Bosideng was under great risk due to overcapacity and high inventories. During the period from 2013 to 2016, the entire garment industry suffered from a great depression, Bosideng was no exception. Its operating revenue dropped from nearly CNY 10 billion to less than CNY 6 billion. In 2014, under the overall situation of slowdown of macroeconomic growth, overall decline of garment industry, and intensified market competition, the inventory pressure of Bosideng was not mitigated although it made great efforts in expanding the marketing channels. The net profit in 2016 was merely CNY 138 million. Meanwhile, the stock price of Bosideng also dropped from around HK$4 per share to around HK$0.4. Under such situations, Bosideng had to change its corporate strategy.

2. The Second Entrepreneurship

In 2018, Bosideng engaged external strategic consulting to systematically analyze and re-examine its characteristics and traditional strategies and decided to initiate a comprehensive strategic transformation. As compared with peer companies, the brand advantages

Case 14 Strategic Entrepreneurship of Bosideng–A Domestic Brand in Down Garment Industry | 257

of Bosideng lied in its leading technical strength accumulated for years and its widely recognized brand reputation. In terms of customers' awareness, Bosideng has become synonymous with the down garment category. This was just the core advantage of Bosideng. In terms of R&D, Bosideng has led three revolutions in the down garment industry since 1976, with its excellent product production technology. Bosideng was granted a total of 177 patents and participated in the development of 5 international standards, 9 national standards and 4 industrial standards. Its strong scientific and technological research and development capabilities can provide important support for improvement of its product quality.

Around the core strategy of "focusing on the main business and main brand", Bosideng, who was determined to change, took a series of practical measures including activating the brand, upgrading products, and optimizing channels.

Bosideng started to re-examine and establish its brand public relations activities and products, adjust its promotion rhythm of marketing activities, and invest its resources mainly in the newly developed products and core flagship products every year. Down garments were functional products, which should represent the trend of fashion while keeping people warm. Therefore, Bosideng launched a number of series of down garments, e.g. Milan Fashion Week series, co-branded IP series, etc. On July 18, 2018, Bosideng held a press conference at the Water Cube in Beijing with huge expenses and became the only brand in the clothing industry listed in the National Brand Program.

Bosideng also kept a high profile and took active measures to promote brand internationalization, bringing excellent design and elegant Chinese elements to the international stage. With high-quality design, forward-looking artistic aesthetics and avant-garde fashion sense, Bosideng showed the world the strong self-confidence and fashion attitude of Chinese clothing brands. For example, in 2018, Bosideng, as an independent brand, was invited to participate in the New York Fashion Week. It held a new product launch show to change consumers' inherent perception towards the brand. This international show sparked heated discussions about Bosideng in the industry, media and consumers around the world, and received positive comments from the media and consumers.

Around the brand positioning, Bosideng made changes in product, sales channels and operations. In terms of product development, Bosideng strengthened inter-departmental communications according to market trends, consumer needs and the brand strategy of Bosideng to ensure the direction of product R&D is in line with the brand strategy of the company. In terms of product innovation, Bosideng established a new quality upgrade committee to exercise control over the R&D, technology, sales and after-sales services. Bosideng attached great importance to product development and upgrading to comprehensively improve the quality and process of fabrics, down, wool, and auxiliary materials on the basis of existing products. For example, Bosideng launched its "Ji Han" series of high-end functional down garments.

In order to optimize its retail network, Bosideng closed the inefficient stores to improve the efficiency of individual stores. Since March 31, 2017, the total number of down garment retail stores increased from 221 to 4,513, the number of directly managed retail outlets increased from 58 to 1,432, and the number of retail outlets operated by third-party distributors increased from 163 to 3,081. Meanwhile, Bosideng continued to increase its support for terminal stores and franchisees, and transformed and upgraded the terminal stores to enhance the shopping experience of consumers. For store design, which was ignored before, Bosideng hired a top design team in French to redesign the stores to build sensory experience for the consumers in Bosideng. Offline stores play an important role for the consumers to recognize the brand, feel the products, and complete the closed-loop consumption. At present, Bosideng has opened stores in many mainstream commercial complexes such as Hangzhou Tower, CapitaLand, Vientiane, and Xintiandi.

Furthermore, Bosideng boldly explored digital operations and made layout of future new scenarios in advance. In the year of 2020 when the COVID-19 epidemic broke out, the operation of offline stores were greatly impacted and the logistics and distribution were

Case 14 Strategic Entrepreneurship of Bosideng–A Domestic Brand in Down Garment Industry

restricted to a large extent. All industries suffered decline of operating income. Faced with this situation, Bosideng made a rapid adjustment to itself. It actively transformed to digital business to focus on new retail capacity building, product rapid reaction capacity building, and data center building, and promoted the application of digital technologies in the operation management process of users, brand, products, channels, retail, human resources and finance. Through digitalization, Bosideng opened a channel for interaction between production and sales and could obtain precise consumption information of consumers to conduct targeted marketing, thus effectively played the role of digital empowerment for brand value growth.

3. Rise Again

Taking "the world's best-selling down garment expert" as the new direction of its competition strategy, Bosideng activated the intrinsic drive of the brand, but also made contribution to the overall upgrade of products and channel, turned the table and achieved steady growth. According to the survey, before 2017, Bosideng's customer group under 30 ages old accounted for less than 11%, which, however, had increased to nearly 30% in 2019. Bosideng made a successful transformation toward a young and fashion brand. In 2020, Bosideng's operating income exceeded CNY12.19 billion, a record high with the year-on-year increase of 17.4%. The sales of down garment ranked first in the world and its gross profit increased from CNY5.51 billion to CNY 6.71 billion at an increase of 21.7%.

【Case 14】

Questions:

1. How did Bosideng discover and seize its entrepreneurial opportunities?

2. How did Bosideng develop internal entrepreneurship?

3. What is the role of strategic entrepreneurship in helping Bosideng create value?

Tips for Answering the Questions:

1. Entrepreneurial opportunities refer to situations where new products and services can meet market demand. Entrepreneurial opportunities may arise in different ways, such as the opportunity to develop and sell new products, or the opportunity to sell existing products in new markets. In this case, Bosideng has entrepreneurial consciousness, is good at finding and grasping entrepreneurial opportunities, and has achieved great commercial success. The question can be analyzed from two perspectives: identifying existing entrepreneurial opportunities and developing new entrepreneurial opportunities.

2. Corporate entrepreneurship refers to the process in which corporate discovers new opportunities, takes advantage of new opportunities and creates new value. In this case, Bosideng carried out a series of top-down and bottom-up internal entrepreneurial actions in order to get rid of the increasingly fierce homogeneous competition dilemma. The question can be analyzed from the perspective of spontaneous strategic behavior and guiding strategic behavior.

3. Strategic entrepreneurship can be either incremental innovation or breakthrough innovation. In this case, Bosideng has more incremental innovation and less breakthrough innovation. However, breakthrough innovation can create more sales revenue and profits, especially greater value for customers, shareholders and other stakeholders. The question can be analyzed according to the type of strategic entrepreneurship which promotes Bosideng to create value.